Psychology in prisons

Prisons have a very distinctive environment; one in which particular psychological problems occur with exaggerated frequency and intensity. If prison staff are to work effectively they must be aware of the influence of this unique environment upon the behaviour of those who inhabit it.

Psychology in Prisons argues that, by applying psychological principles, behaviour within prisons can be better understood, and violence, distress and stress can be limited. The authors show how psychology can be used to increase our understanding of prisoners, how they became involved in crime, and how they adapt to prison life. They explain how psychology can be used and applied to make for more effective day-to-day dealing with prisoners. The authors focus on key areas of tension and particular problem groups, including sex offenders, violent offenders and the issue of AIDS. But the book also considers how working in prison affects its staff and explores how they can use psychological principles both to reduce the level of stress they undergo in their work and to secure the prisoners' mental well-being.

Psychology in Prisons will be of interest to those with a broad interest in applied psychology or to anyone who is involved with work in prisons.

Psychology in prisons

David J. Cooke,
Pamela J. Baldwin

and

Jacqueline Howison

London and New York

First published 1990
by Routledge
11 New Fetter Lane, London EC4P 4EE

Simultaneously published in the USA and Canada
by Routledge
29 West 35th Street, New York, NY 10001

First published in paperback by Routledge in 1993

Transferred to Digital Printing 2003

© 1990 David Cooke, Pamela Baldwin and Jacqueline Howison

Typeset by LaserScript Limited, Mitcham, Surrey

British Library Cataloguing in Publication Data

Cooke, David, *1952–*
    Psychology in prisons.
    1. Prison life. Psychological aspects
    I. Baldwin, Pamela, *1954–*   II. Howison, Jacqueline, *1956–*
365′.4′019

Library of Congress Cataloging in Publication Data

Cooke, David.
    Psychology in prisons / David Cooke, Pamela Baldwin,
    and Jacqueline Howison.
    p. cm.
    1. Prison psychology. I. Baldwin, Pamela (Pamela J.)
    II. Howison, Jacqueline. III. Title.
    HV6089.C66 1990   90-8226
    365′.6′019—dc20   CIP

ISBN 0-415-00533-7
ISBN 0-415-09714-2 (pbk)

Contents

1   **Psychology and its role in prisons**   1
    Isn't everyone a psychologist?   2
    Psychology and its role in prisons   2
    Psychology in prisons: the layout of this book   5

2   **Criminal behaviour – how it develops**   8
    Early environment   9
    Heredity   10
    Socio-economic status   10
    Current living circumstances   11
    Crises and negative events   11
    Summary   15

3   **Understanding sex offenders**   16
    The development of sexual interests   16
    Differences in sexual attitudes   18
    Indecent exposure   19
    Sexual assault and rape   20
    Sexual offences involving children   21
    Incest   22
    Homosexuality   23
    Prostitution   24
    Sex offenders in prison   25
    Summary   26

4   **Alcohol and drugs – their role in criminal behaviour**   27
    Good and bad drugs: good and bad uses   27
    Types of drug   28

Contents

Alcohol, drugs and crime   35
Coming off drugs   36
Reducing the risks   39
Alcohol and drug use in prison staff   40
Summary   40

5 Understanding violence and aggression   42
   Key words   42
   Kinds of aggression   42
   Learning aggression with a purpose   43
   Gains from aggression   45
   What makes people aggressive?   45
   Summary   53

6 Psychological disturbance in prison   55
   Loss of control   55
   Loss of family   56
   Lack of stimulation   58
   Loss of models   60
   Psychological disturbance   60
   Summary   66

7 The impact of AIDS on prison life   67
   What is AIDS?   68
   How AIDS is passed on   68
   Fear of infection   69
   Who is at risk?   69
   How can we know who is infected?   71
   Detecting the AIDS virus   71
   What the HIV test can and cannot tell   72
   How do we tell when someone has AIDS?   73
   How can we protect ourselves?   73
   Taking precautions   74
   Controlling AIDS   75
   The prisoner and AIDS   76
   Summary   77

8 Communication skills   79
   Improving communication skills   79
   What communication skills are important in prisons? 80

Giving orders   88
Handling requests   89
Writing reports   89
Summary   90

9 **Coping with disturbed prisoners**   92
Describing psychological disturbance   92
Prisoners with learning difficulties   98
Brain damage   100
Summary   101

10 **Coping with face-to-face violence**   102
Avoiding the problem   102
Motives and emotions of aggressors   104
Taking precautions   104
Facing aggressive people   106
Avoid escalation   106
Behaviour in the violent situation   108
Staff issues   110
Summary   111

11 **Hostage-taking in prisons**   112
The history of hostage-taking   112
Methods of resolving hostage-taking   113
Hostage-taking in British prisons   115
Coping with hostage-taking – first on the scene   116
Coping with hostage-taking – being a hostage   117
Coping with hostage-taking – the aftermath   120
Coping with hostage-taking – other staff   121
Summary   122

12 **Stress and working in prisons**   123
The effects of stress   124
Why are prisons stressful places?   126
The need for an optimum level of pressure   128
Coping with stress   128
Strategies for stress prevention   129
Skills for managing stress   131
Summary   136

Contents

13 Giving evidence in court   137
Going to court   139
Giving evidence   140
Types of evidence-giving   140
Summary   145

Index   146

Chapter one

Psychology and its role in prisons

To do their job, and indeed sometimes in order to survive, all prison officers need to use some psychology. Many do this from years of experience or from well-developed instincts. In this book we will describe psychological ideas and techniques which may be of some value in the day-to-day tasks of the prison officer. We hope that it will help staff to understand the usual and unusual behaviour of prisoners; to help them to deal with the aggression, the distress and the difficulties of the prisoners in their charge. We hope to demonstrate that it is helpful to look at prisoners as individuals rather than a mass of stereotypes and that it is useful to try to observe prisoners' behaviour and work out what makes them tick.

Think about disruptive prisoners; they are not all alike: some are disruptive because they are bloody-minded, others in order to achieve status, some just to break the monotony of prison life, yet others as a cry for help. You will know examples of the individual who lashes out at other prisoners to show his strength, the prisoner who breaks up his cell so that he will be put in isolation and the young man who takes a hostage because he is bored. It can be seen that the psychology behind these various disruptive acts is different. To understand, control and manage prisoners we have to understand their motivation, their thought processes and their individual approach to life.

This is just a taste of why we think that psychology should be of interest to people who work in prisons. We hope that we can show that psychology can be used to make the job of the prison officer easier and provide more job satisfaction.

1

Isn't everyone a psychologist?

Isn't everyone a bit of a psychologist? Don't we all study the behaviour of others and try to predict what they will do next? We spend our lives predicting; predicting whether an angry prisoner is going to become violent, whether our superior is going to believe why we are late, whether someone is friendly or hostile, whether the other driver will cut in front of us. We all study behaviour. We all make predictions. However, we are not all practising psychology. A basic principle of psychological science is that the study of behaviour should be exact and systematic. It is also the study of how things happen (the 'process'), for example, how and why an angry prisoner becomes violent, whether this will happen and the thought processes that lead up to it. The amateur psychologist may have 'gut feelings' about a person or a prisoner and he may be right, but he will not be able to identify the processes which lead to this view. Many people are good at describing other people, but their descriptions are not systematic, nor are they always complete. This means that their descriptions cannot be analysed, described or conveyed to other people. It is like the explorer who can find his way unaided through the Amazonian jungle. He may possess a useful skill, but its value is limited if he cannot convey his knowledge to other people. Others cannot benefit or learn from his skill. So if we have no 'map' of psychological process we cannot check to see if it is really the best way to do something, we cannot fully understand the process. The professional psychologist tries to map the 'gut reactions' of the non-psychologist, he tries to work out the rules which influence the behaviour of people. With this type of information it is often possible to either explain or predict the behaviour of individual people. This is the aim of the professional psychologist.

Psychology and its role in prisons

So what are psychologists interested in and why might this be of interest to people who work in prisons? These are the questions which we will try to answer in this book. In this first chapter we will look at what psychologists do and what they study, and try to show that psychological ideas can help people in their day-to-day work with prisoners.

There are many definitions of psychology and what it is about, but the most straightforward one is that 'Psychology is the study of brain and behaviour'. What does this mean? Psychologists are interested in how the brain works. They study the processes whereby the light which passes into our eyes is turned into colour, movement and shapes. They investigate how we remember what we hear or see. They analyse how we learn and how we use language and so on and so forth. Equally, psychologists are interested in behaviour so they may be able to predict what will calm a violent person. They may monitor the way that group pressure affects what you decide to do. They may explain why a disturbed child continues to bang its head on a wall. Unlike psychiatry, which is mainly concerned with medical problems, disordered brains and behaviour, psychology is concerned with the whole range of human activity, the normal as well as the abnormal. The subject of psychology is now so large that psychologists have to specialise in small areas. It might give a clearer picture if we look at what the different types of psychologist do or study.

Psychologists can be divided into those who apply psychology and those who do research and have an academic interest. We will start by looking at the applied psychologists.

There are four main types of applied psychologist: clinical, educational, occupational and sports psychologists. They all work in different settings and although they all know about 'brain and behaviour', they apply this knowledge to the particular problems which they come across in their specialist fields.

What do clinical psychologists do? Clinical psychologists usually work with people who have psychological difficulties in their everyday life and with those who help them. Their clients may be anxious or depressed, they may have learning difficulties, they may be suffering from brain damage or they may have been in hospital so long that they have lost the ability to survive on their own. If a person is anxious the clinical psychologist will use his knowledge of 'brain and behaviour' to help them reduce their anxiety. If the person is anxious about talking to other people they will be taught basic social skills; how to start a conversation, how to be a good listener or how to stand up for their rights. These are skills that we all find useful; prison officers can use the same skills to improve their management of prisoners (Chapter 8).

Clinical psychologists are interested not just in those people who are clearly disturbed but also in psychological problems of any degree, large or small. They are also concerned about preventing difficulties from arising in certain situations. For example, a prison can be a difficult place in which to work and it can create problems of anxiety and depression. The skills which clinical psychologists teach patients can be

3

usefully applied by any prison officer who is under stress (see Chapter 12).

Educational psychologists work with schoolchildren, in particular, those with special educational needs. They might test a child to find out why he is unable to read. The educational psychologist will then advise the teacher how to structure his lessons in order that the child might learn this skill more easily. If a child is disrupting the class, then the teacher will be advised on how to alter the way he controls the child to stop the child being disruptive.

Occupational psychologists are found in many work places, in factories, offices, and even in prisons. Occupational psychologists apply their knowledge of psychology to help people cope effectively and efficiently with work. Occupational psychologists might help design aircraft controls so that the pilot is not given too much information at one time. They may design ways of selecting the right people for particular jobs or occupations. A good example of this activity is the new selection procedure for prison officers in England. To begin with, psychologists assessed the many jobs which prison officers undertake. They looked at 28 different types of job and systematically measured the skills, aptitudes and personal qualities needed to carry them out. They found that prison officers had to be alert, vigilant and observant; they had to be able to make decisions quickly and communicate fluently and accurately. These were the important skills and aptitudes. The personal qualities which were important included being considerate towards others, being reliable and possessing a sense of responsibility. Other qualities seen as useful in a prison officer were having a sense of humour, being confident and assertive without being aggressive, and being able to tolerate strained relationships and conflicts.

Discovering the skills, aptitudes and personal qualities required to be a good prison officer was only the first part of the task. Once they had identified these qualities they designed paper-and-pencil tests and an interview to detect people with these qualities.

Occupational psychologists design assessment procedures for all sorts of occupations, even for the SAS. When assessing soldiers for their suitability for the SAS, psychologists look for individuals who are above average in intelligence, assertive and self-sufficient. They do not look for extremely stable individuals, but rather for people who are forthright and not dependent on orders.

Sports psychologists and their work emphasise the point that psychologists are interested in all human behaviour, not just abnormal behaviour. It is widely recognised that with top level athletes or sportsmen the level of skill, fitness and physical prowess is often similar. The small difference between the good and the great sportsmen is psychological: the difference is in the individual's concentration, motivation and belief in themselves. When John Betrand won the America's Cup for Australia, breaking the longest winning run in sporting history, he used a sports psychologist. This psychologist helped him detect the strengths and weaknesses in his crew and taught them how to go through the pain barrier. He helped Betrand to control his explosive temper because temper outbursts distracted him from sailing the boat. He also taught Betrand the techniques of mental visualisation: Betrand had to get through the psychological barrier that no challenger had won the America's Cup in the previous 132 years. By repeatedly visualising himself in front of the American boat and crossing the line first, he built up his self-confidence and broke through this psychological block. These techniques can be used whenever we have a challenge to face, be it a promotion board, having to negotiate in a hostage situation or trying to quell a prison riot. Psychological techniques are now used routinely in a wide range of sports from football and basketball to tennis, golf, track events and downhill skiing.

We have looked at some of the activities of applied psychologists. Applied psychologists depend on other psychologists, the academic psychologists, to develop ever more detailed understanding of 'brain and behaviour'. What do academic psychologists do?

As with applied psychology, academic psychologists specialise. Some will study personality and intelligence, some will study how children develop language, others will study how we remember or how brain cells detect the different shapes which we see, still others will study the signals or 'body language' which we use when we are communicating. The range of topics is endless.

Psychology in prisons: the layout of this book

This book is in two sections. In the first five chapters we look at some of the reasons why people commit the crimes which result in them receiving prison sentences – the origins of criminal behaviour. How important is the prisoner's early development? Is material deprivation important? How important is parental love, discipline and violence? Do criminals learn to be criminals from their parents or from their friends? All these questions will be explored in the second chapter.

Sex offenders often have a difficult time when they are in prison, and in the third chapter we will describe some of the reasons why people rape, expose themselves or engage in sadistic behaviour.

While alcohol has always had a role in criminal behaviour, drugs and solvents are now also having an important impact. In the fourth chapter we look at some basic facts about drink and drugs and at why people drink, what alcohol does to someone and what is a safe level of drinking. We will look at the long term effects of drinking. These will include physical and psychological effects as well as the effects it may have on family and friends. We will look at similar effects from the use of drugs and solvents.

Dealing with violent behaviour is one of the most dangerous and difficult parts of the job for any prison officer and in the fifth chapter we look at different types of violence. Some people may be violent because their sub-culture demands it, others are violent because they are trying to get something for themselves, others are violent because they are naturally very angry and cannot control this anger. In the fifth chapter we look at how violence develops and the factors which promote and diffuse it.

It is becoming more widely realised that prison officers have to deal with people who are psychologically disturbed. Some prisoners may be psychologically disturbed when they come into jail, others become disturbed while they serve their sentence. Some become disturbed because of the experience of imprisonment and others because of problems affecting their families outside. In the sixth chapter we will examine what effects being imprisoned can have.

The close association between drug abuse and HIV infection means that prison officers will have to understand and assist prisoners who are suffering from AIDS. In the seventh chapter we provide basic advice on the nature of AIDS and HIV infection and examine some of the psychological effects for the infected and those working with them.

In the first section of the book we try to show how psychology can be used to increase our understanding of prisoners, how they became involved in crime, how they cope and adapt to prison life. In the second half of the book we try to show how psychology can be used or applied to make us more effective in the day-to-day job of dealing with prisoners.

Prison officers need to be alert and observant. More and more they are expected to write down their observations in reports. In Chapter 8 we show that observed behaviour can be analysed systematically and precisely and how behaviour can be described in a concrete, systematic and objective fashion. We will also demonstrate how such descriptions can make report writing less of a chore and make the reports of greater value. Many of the difficulties in the prison system can be reduced by good communication between staff and inmates. In the chapter we also look at communication skills. We show how a prison officer can calm an angry or distressed prisoner by using the skills of the 'good listener'. We describe how a prison officer can get his view across in an assertive rather than an aggressive manner and we look at the problem of giving orders effectively.

We start Chapter 9 by looking at the psychological effects of being imprisoned and we describe the signs which tell whether someone is depressed or anxious. We consider why people might be driven to take or even attempt to take their own lives, and we describe the methods that a skilled officer can use to alleviate some of the psychological pressures on prisoners in his charge. In Chapter 10, we look at how to prevent face-to-face violence. The experienced prison officer can often pick up instinctively changes which are likely to lead to violence. We discuss the signs to look out for so that early action in such a situation can be taken. In the next chapter, we look at one of the most extreme forms of violence that can occur in a prison, the taking of a hostage. We will describe what the hostage-taker is likely to do and what you should do if you are taken hostage.

People are beginning to recognise that the work which prison staff undertake can be stressful. In Chapter 12 we examine stress and describe how to recognise it and what you can do to avoid or manage it. By applying the ideas we discuss earlier in the book, we hope you can make your job less stressful.

More and more prison officers have to appear in court to give evidence about offences that they have witnessed during the course of their work. Giving evidence can be an unnerving experience. There are skills that can be learned which make the experience less unnerving and your evidence sound more convincing.

There is a lot more to psychology than it is possible to cram into this small book. However, we hope that we can demonstrate the value of psychology in prisons, and that you will find it useful.

Chapter two

Criminal behaviour – how it develops

Many people who work with offenders often wonder why individuals first enter into crime, and why they keep offending. This seems especially curious if the offender keeps being punished by imprisonment or fines. It hardly seems worth it. So why do some people become criminals? Is it merely because they are evil, wicked or bad – or is it more complicated than that?

The first thing to say is that criminals are all different, so they are all likely to offend for different reasons: there is no one simple explanation for criminal behaviour. Someone who steals cars to go joy-riding has a different reason for committing that crime than the man who embezzles thousands of pounds in a computer fraud. In the first case, the offender is likely to be someone who seeks excitement from the thrill of taking and driving away. He (since it is usually a man) will probably come across an opportunity that he just cannot resist, and he will act impulsively. In the second case, the offender is likely to be someone who has carefully planned the fraud over a long period of time and who is intent on gradually and systematically acquiring large sums of money. They are very different crimes and very different criminals.

What we know about crime and criminals is based on people who are caught, and convicted. This can distort the picture. We should not forget that many people break the law every day and do not get caught; some by not declaring their full income to the Inland Revenue, some by theft from their place of work, others by driving with more alcohol in their blood than is permitted by law. We all know people who break the law, but who are never arrested. They are classed as non-criminal. Others who commit the same offences, but are caught, are classed as 'criminals'. Thus being defined as a criminal is a bit haphazard. Most people commit offences at some time in their lives but they do not all get caught. Rather than look at what produces criminals it is better to look at what leads to criminal behaviour.

Why do people behave in a criminal way? This is an age-old question for which we do not have the answer. However, there are some clues. There are three sets of factors which can have a bearing on whether someone indulges in criminal behaviour or not. The first set includes early influences, for example upbringing and heredity. The second set includes the offender's current circumstances, where he lives, whether he is employed or not, and crises in his live. The third set of factors includes the circumstances immediately prior to the offence, what the offender was feeling, what he was thinking, how risky the offence is, how easy it is to commit. To understand criminal behaviour we have to consider all these factors; different factors will be important for different people.

Early environment

A person's early environment can set them off along the path towards criminality. We all know of prisoners who started getting into trouble the minute they walked into primary school at the age of five. Certain experiences appear to be important. It is almost a cliché that criminals come from a 'broken home'. It is true that a lot of criminals come from homes where their parents were separated or divorced. There is some truth in this view but what seems to be more important is the quality of the relationship that the child has with his parents. A child needs to experience warmth and care from his parents and this emotional closeness must be consistent. Furthermore, if parents have few rules about how their child should behave, if they let their child go about unsupervised, and if they do not exercise any control or discipline, then the chances of the child getting into delinquent habits are much greater. All children copy their parents' behaviour to some extent. If their father gets into fights, breaks into houses, steals cars or sells heroin, then these forms of criminal behaviour are seen as normal by the children. We should not be surprised if they copy this behaviour.

Many prison officers seem to doubt the importance of early environment: 'I was brought up in the Gorbals, I didn't become a gangster.' This raises two important points. First, as we have seen, it is the quality of your upbringing – how your parents looked after you – rather than where you were brought up which seems to matter. Second, some people seem

9

to be vulnerable to bad influences. Some people who are exposed to bad influences are unaffected by them, others – the vulnerable people – start breaking the law. This often puzzles people. They think that if a 'bad upbringing' doesn't always cause people to become criminals, then you cannot really regard it as a cause – 'I came from a violent home but I didn't go around assaulting people – people who say it's their upbringing are just making an excuse'. Human behaviour is complex. Some people are vulnerable to particular influences, others are not. Let us take a simple example. Polio is caused by a viral infection. However, only 5 per cent of people with the infection actually develop the full symptomatology. No one would deny that polio is caused by a virus, but it only affects people who are vulnerable to the virus. Criminal behaviour may well be the same.

Heredity

It is difficult to unravel the influence of heredity from the influence of early upbringing. Does a son follow in his father's criminal footsteps because he inherited his father's criminal tendencies or because he copied his father's criminal behaviour? There is little evidence to support the idea that people inherit criminal tendencies. The most popular genetic theory of recent years was the XYY theory. It was thought that having an extra Y chromosome made men become aggressive psychopaths. However, careful analysis showed that you could not distinguish between the behaviour of 'normal' men and the behaviour of XYY men.

Socio-economic status

Criminal behaviour seemed to be linked to who you are and where you live. Males get involved in crime more often than women. Eight times as many men as women are prosecuted in Scotland every year. Twenty-eight times as many men as women are in prison in Scotland. Generally, crime is committed by young unskilled males. When they are unemployed they are more likely to commit crimes than when they are in employment. It is not hard to see why. When they are unemployed they have more opportunity to commit crime; they may use crime, not only as a way of obtaining money and material comforts, but also as a means of combating boredom.

Current living circumstances

How you are living and where you are living seem to affect criminal behaviour. If you live in the inner city, have associates who are delinquent, if you have little to do and nowhere to go other than the street, then acts of vandalism may seem easy to commit.

Crises and negative events

We now know that crises and negative events in our lives can cause all sorts of psychological problems. Negative events can trigger problems from anxiety and depression through the common cold, appendicitis and ulcers to heart attacks and menstrual problems. Perhaps surprisingly, negative events can also lead to offending. Consider a real example.

Mrs X was caught shop-lifting. The security personnel in the supermarket noticed that she was carrying a shopping bag as well as the supermarket basket. They saw her put a pound of butter, a packet of cheese and a tin of hamburgers into her bag. She was found to have twenty-one pounds in her purse. The Procurator-fiscal sent her along to see a psychologist because he thought that her behaviour was totally out of character. She told the psychologist that in the two years prior to the offence she had experienced a series of tragedies and problems:

1) her husband was housebound because of chronic cardiac problems and diabetes,
2) a favourite uncle, in whom she could confide, died unexpectedly,
3) a son-in-law cut his throat in an attempt to kill himself,
4) another son-in-law jumped from the top landing of a prison wing and is now paraplegic,
5) one daughter had a miscarriage and was hospitalised,
6) another daughter moved away from home to live with a heroin addict,
7) another daughter (16 years of age) was pregnant and she was not sure whether to marry the father or not.

Mrs X's explanation for the offence was that she had been worried about her pregnant daughter and she was scared to tell her husband in case he had a heart attack. She said that she was hurrying round the supermarket and had run out of space in her basket so she put the additional goods in her bag with the intention of paying for them. She got distracted by her worries and forgot to pay for them. Mrs X may have been lying but the way she told her story suggested that she was being truthful. In studies of shop-lifters who claim they have been wrongly convicted, many suggest that they were confused or absent-minded. Before dismissing such claims as excuses, try to remember, have you ever acted in an absent-minded way in a shop? Have you walked out without paying for something, have you walked away from the check-out without picking up your change, have you gone to a shop to buy a specific item and come away without it? Most people have. In a study of people who had not been accused of shop-lifting or any other offence, 18 per cent said that they had accidentally left a shop with an article for which they had not paid.

If we move on to the third set of factors – those immediately before the offence – we see that there are psychological factors, including the person's reasons for committing this particular offence, and there are the 'situational' factors, for example, how easy it is to break into the house.

The reasons for committing criminal acts are many and varied. There are obvious ones such as the bank robber who steals for material gain, the 'junkie' who mugs so that he can buy heroin, the youth who joins in the gang fight so that he does not lose face with his friends and the drunk who exposes himself because he is so disinhibited by the effects of alcohol. These examples are commonplace; however, other reasons are perhaps less obvious. Sadistic murderers do not kill because they are drunk and angry but because they need to feel in total control over their victim. The act of killing makes them feel invulnerable and in control. In a less extreme form certain criminals commit criminal acts so that they can feel that they have achieved something positive, they have mastered the obstacles which they feel that society has put in their way. Some people commit offences as a way of reducing their tension. Both within and outside prison, individuals who get uptight and tense may set fires as a means of getting rid of the uncomfortable physical and psychological symptoms of anxiety. They will report that they experienced a feeling of relaxation and general well-being after they set the fire.

Human behaviour being complex, people do not always commit offences just for one reason. The picture is often more complicated. A real life example may illustrate this point. A bank robber was going shopping with his wife and on passing a bank he developed a powerful urge to rob it. He stopped his car, removed a gun from the boot of his car and went ahead with the robbery. He reported that immediately afterwards he felt 'on top of the world' and that he got a 'buzz' which was stronger than that which he got when he went rock-climbing or parachuting. From his account it would appear that there were many reasons for the offence. The act was impulsive – he was taking his wife shopping – but it gave him excitement, he felt in control and superior to the 'mugs' around him, it boosted his self-esteem. He also made substantial financial gains. Many offences are less complex than this but it is not uncommon for there to be more than one reason for an offence.

It is not only psychological reasons that lead people to offend. What is going on around them – their circumstances – also affects whether they offend or not. Let's consider two murders. A well-adjusted 'normal' man returns home and finds an intruder raping his wife, he picks up a kitchen knife and repeatedly stabs the intruder until he is dead. Psychologically, this individual was not prone to anger or aggression; however, under these extreme circumstances he acted with extreme violence. Contrast this with the case of the angry volatile man who was asked to move aside in a pub and who stabbed his victim in response to a mild and reasonable request. In the first case, external circumstances were of great importance; in the second, the psychological factors – the anger and volatility – were the more important.

However, to understand any offence we must understand the way in which the psychological factors and the circumstances go together to produce the offence. Circumstances not only affect whether someone commits an offence or not, but also the form the offence takes. The unemployed youth with little to do and nowhere to go may be prone to vandalism, the distressed woman who shops in a supermarket rather than a small grocer's is more likely to commit shop-lifting, the dishonest computer expert with access to a bank's computer is more likely to turn to computer fraud than armed robbery.

The description we have given of factors that lead to criminal behaviour may make you think that we believe people have no control over whether they commit crimes. That is not true. People usually – but not always – make a decision about whether to commit a crime or not.

For many kinds of behaviour – including criminal behaviour – 'cost-benefit analysis' can be done. By this, we mean that you can weigh up the cost to yourself of doing something, and beside that you estimate the benefit you get out of it. Here are some examples:

Activity	Cost	Benefit
Taking my son to the cinema	I have to sit through an hour and a half of boring cartoons when I'd rather be playing golf £3.25 for the tickets	My son is really happy He is good-natured for the rest of the day. Seeing him happy makes me feel good

In this case you are likely to weigh up the costs of taking your son to the cinema and the benefits, and probably decide to take him because the benefits outweigh the costs.

Activity	Cost	Benefit
Going for a drink after work	I'll be late home for tea and that will cause a bad atmosphere all evening	It'll be a good laugh

In this case you may decide that the cost of going for a drink, in terms of the row at home, is not worth the benefit of going to the pub. On another occasion, you may just go to the pub because your cost-benefit analysis comes out with the other solution.

Someone who commits a crime is also making a cost-benefit analysis, but the importance they attach to the factors involved may be different from the importance that you would attach. This might just be as a result of their personality, or the way in which they were brought up in the family or their particular neighbourhood. An example might be:

Activity	Cost	Benefit
Breaking into two houses for a video, jewellery, and cash	The chance of being caught	A video and other goods which can be sold for around £400

If the thief thinks that there is a great risk of being caught and that this will result in imprisonment, then the cost will outweigh the benefit. So he is unlikely to do it. But if he thinks that it is unlikely that he will be caught, or if he does not even think at all about being caught, then the

£400 will be his only consideration and he will break into the houses. Since a large number of housebreakers are never caught, many of them will rate the risk, or 'cost', as low and not very important.

Many people convicted of crimes such as housebreaking do not think a great deal about the consequences of their crime. They rarely think that they will be caught. If they did think long and hard about the consequences of their crime in terms of the fine or imprisonment, then the cost might outweigh the benefit and they would probably not do it.

In our cost-benefit analysis, if you come from a background where there is little hope of a job or of getting a nice home or of having much money, then the attraction of stealing money is more likely to outweigh the risk of going into prison. The life of some young offenders seems to be so hopeless outside that the threat of imprisonment seems to be limited. Some will tell you that at least in prison they get three meals a day, they can mix with their pals and they have a routine. Their liberty seems to have a low value. It is not surprising that the outcome of their cost-benefit analyses is different to that of the majority of people.

Summary

Our understanding of crime and criminals is based on people who are caught. This may be a distorted picture because many people who break the law are not caught. If we are to begin to understand why someone commits a crime we need to understand a range of factors including their early experience, their current life circumstances and the circumstances immediately prior to the offence. Different factors will be important for different crimes and different criminals.

Chapter three

Understanding sex offenders

Judging from the newspapers, other people's sexual behaviour is of great interest to us. This interest includes some of the more unusual forms of sexual behaviour. Journalists often describe these unusual forms with extraordinary headlines. These headlines grab our attention and we hurry to read and be shocked, excited or amused.

'RENT BOY SHAME OF FORMER MP'
'TAKE ME BACK SAYS REF IN SEX PROBE'
'SPANKING COLONEL IN SEX SCANDAL'

Many people might say that such sensational sexual activities are not 'normal'. But it is unlikely that these same people, if completely honest, would want to describe their own sexual thoughts, fantasies or activities. This is because sexual behaviour is extremely variable and many people's fantasies may be a little peculiar. Every man and woman has their own preferences or feelings about sexual behaviour, and they are all different.

Before we go on to describe various types of sexual behaviour – sexual behaviour which can lead to criminal charges – we should first look at how sexual interests develop.

The development of sexual interests

How do sexual interests develop? Some people argue that sexual preferences are learned, others that people are born 'programmed' to have particular preferences.

Some people argue that children generally learn by observation, instruction and example to be attracted to members of the opposite sex.

Men become attracted to women because such attraction is shown on television, in books, and in real life around them. When this learning process breaks down, perhaps because of the unusual sexual behaviour of the child's parents, the child may develop unusual sexual interests.

More specific learning experiences may be important. There is some evidence that the experience which first produces strong sexual arousal may set the individual on the path of having unusual sexual preferences. One patient who developed a strong fetish about incontinence bags reported that the first time he masturbated to climax was when he was looking at pictures of disabled people. His sexual interest in disability and the aids of the disabled was still present twenty years later.

In most cases one event is probably not sufficient to 'imprint' deviant sexual interests. Rubber fetishists who belonged to the Mackintosh Society appeared to have developed their particular interest between the age of four and ten. For many of them this was during the Second World War, a time when rubber objects including capes, groundsheets and gas masks were in special abundance.

Deviant sexual interests are often developed and maintained through masturbation. People with deviant sexual interest often collect pornography that fits their particular sexual interest in order to use it during masturbation. Repeated masturbation to the deviant material appears to increase the excitement that the fantasies have for the person. In some cases masturbation to pornographic material or deviant fantasies fails to produce enough sexual arousal. Often rapists, child molesters and sexual killers report that they try out their fantasies in the real world. They may start by tracking a woman from a distance and then go home and masturbate to fantasies of raping or murdering her. The excitement produced by this activity will diminish in time and so they may get bolder, getting closer to their prey or even touching them as if by accident. Progressively, their behaviour gets closer to their fantasies until ultimately they commit a serious offence.

Some people think that sexual preferences are 'programmed' biologically and that our brains are normally constructed so that we respond to members of the opposite sex. Just as a baby responds spontaneously to the smiling face of an adult so individuals automatically develop an interest in the opposite sex. But sexual development is more complicated than that.

The arrangement of the chromosomes is the basis for deciding whether a baby will be a boy or a girl: this is not always a simple distinction. Occasionally there are unusual chromosomal arrangements so that the baby is born with some male and some female features. This can cause difficulty for the person as they grow up since both their physical appearance, as well as their hormonal make-up, will be giving confusing messages. This is one explanation for people who change sex in adulthood. In other people, however, a strong desire to change sex without these unusual chromosomal arrangements is developed.

As with all human behaviour it would be wrong to suggest that one explanation – either the biological or the learning explanation – was correct and the other was wrong. Abnormal or unusual sexual interests probably develop from the interplay of biology and experience.

Differences in sexual attitudes

It is important to emphasise that it is almost impossible to define what are normal sexual behaviour and normal sexual attitudes. There are enormous differences between individuals, across cultures and across time. Even our ideas of what is attractive in sexual partners have changed in the last fifty years. In the 1940s and 1950s people used to idolise curvaceous women, like Marilyn Monroe, and broad, well-built men, like Errol Flynn, and then, in the 1960s and 1970s they favoured the tall, very slim figures like Twiggy and David Bowie.

Just as our images of sexy people have changed, so have our notions of sexual behaviour. For example, in Europe, in medieval times, poor health meant that fewer people lived beyond middle age. To fit in with this life expectancy, people often married in their early teens and had children at a much younger age than they do today. In Shakespeare's *Romeo and Juliet*, Juliet was less than fourteen years old. In the United Kingdom we now have laws which prevent people from marrying below the age of sixteen and a man can be prosecuted for having sexual intercourse with a girl who is under age. These laws are comparatively new. The Victorians raised the age of consent to sixteen to protect young girls from being sold into prostitution by their unscrupulous parents. The age of consent varies across countries. In different States in the USA the age of consent ranges from twelve to eighteen; in France it is fourteen.

In the United Kingdom, homosexual relations with someone under the age of twenty-one is still an offence. In the times of the early Greeks and Romans, people accepted that homosexual relationships often developed between male teachers and their boy pupils. Times have changed, and so have our attitudes towards sex.

People in different countries hold differing views about sex and marriage and these often go with their religious beliefs. In Muslim countries, a man may take more than one wife, quite legally. In some hill tribes in Nepal, a woman may marry two or more brothers. In California, attitudes towards homosexuality have for a long time been more accepting than they are in Europe. In parts of New Guinea young men stay away from women in order to practise sex with other males. They believe that the intake of sperm from a virile older male is essential if they are to become good husbands and good fathers. In some Arab countries, adultery is against the law, and people who commit such a crime can be punished harshly. In some European countries, it used to be against the law, but this is no longer the case. In Eire there are laws to restrict the availability of contraceptive devices; in China contraception is widely encouraged in order to carry out the government's policy that families should restrict themselves to only one child.

So human beings all over the world hold different views about what is 'normal' sex, and often their laws fit in with these views. In this chapter, we look at sexual behaviour that causes problems, either because it breaks the law, breaks prison rules, or causes people distress and unhappiness. Let us consider different forms of sexual offence.

Indecent exposure

In this country, it is an offence to expose the genital area in public. The most common offenders are adult males, aged over twenty-one, although the number of convictions among younger males has been increasing over the last twenty years or so. Many of these adult offenders started exposing themselves when they were adolescents. They are not unusual in terms of the social class that they come from, or the level of intelligence that they have. Many exhibitionists find it very difficult to stop offending, and are convicted of numerous offences.

Many people find it hard to understand why a person would expose themself in public. There seem to be various motives. Most people convicted of indecent exposure are 'exhibitionists', that is, they want to display the genital area to members of the opposite sex, but do not intend to take the behaviour any further. They are unlikely to go on to carry out a sexual assault. It seems that genital exposure is more of a hostile act: the offender wishes the victim to be shocked, afraid or insulted. If this happens, then the offender is likely to feel more powerful and in control of women. The victims are frequently teenage girls, which increases the man's feeling of superiority. Often such men tend not to have much say in the way things are at home. In exposing themselves, it is the feeling of power they are seeking, rather than a sexual contact.

However, a small proportion of people convicted of indecent exposure are seeking sexual pleasure, and will be sexually excited at the time. Some men believe that, by exposing their genitals, they will excite and attract women to engage in sexual intercourse with them. Other men do it because they are drunk, or because they think it is funny and will cause a few laughs.

So there seems to be a range of motives associated with indecent exposure. Some exhibitionists are sexually inhibited or inexperienced; however, many have ordinary sexual relations with their wives or girl-friends. Those offenders who also have ordinary sexual relations will often report that the exhibitionism gives them more intense pleasure than sexual intercourse. That is why they continue to expose themselves. In most cases, the behaviour will not develop into sexual assault, but in some people, it may do so. Obviously this is much more serious. Although indecent exposure is very unpleasant for the victim, it does not seem to cause lasting harm to them. This is not the case with sexual assault, attempted rape, or rape, which usually have very serious and damaging effects on the victims.

Sexual assault and rape

Sexual assault, rape and related offences are amongst the most serious offences, both in terms of the legal consequences for the offender and the psychological consequences for the victim. They are violent offences usually committed by adult males on young females. There are, however, cases of homosexual rape. These are most likely to take place where men are contained together and where there is also an atmosphere of violence. There are a number of reports describing the occurrence of homosexual rape in prisons.

As in the case of indecent exposure, the motives associated with the various types of sexual assault are often to do with aggression rather than sexual pleasure. In other words, where a man sexually assaults another man or a woman, he is often wanting to demonstrate power or masculinity by humiliating the victim. This may be because he cannot be powerful in other areas of his life, or because he has developed a hatred or anger towards the victim, or people like the victim.

Group rape is usually committed by young males who are in a 'gang'. Their victims are often adolescent females whom they may already know. In these cases, not only is the motive one of violence but also to do with doing things in a group. A gang like this may commit other offences such as assault, vandalism and housebreaking in the same way. Most convicted rapists are either in their early twenties or younger. They do not seem to differ from other offenders in terms of intelligence or family background. In about half the cases, rapists' victims are complete strangers, and in the other half, the victims are known to the offenders, either neighbours, friends or relatives. Often the offender has been drinking at the time of the offence.

Many victims are afraid of reporting rape to the police. They fear that they will not be believed. Another worry is that they will have to go through the ordeals of medical examinations, police questioning and court appearances. Not only will this mean that they will have to go through the whole experience again when it is described, but it might be suggested that they are not telling the truth. This means that official statistics on the number of rapes that take place and the circumstances in which they occur are likely to be incomplete.

Victims of sexual assault are often put in an impossible situation: if they are injured or threatened with violence they are likely to be very afraid of being murdered. Under this threat, it may be best to offer little resistance to the attacker in the hope that he will not inflict further injury. Yet if they receive few injuries, there is a risk that others will not believe them. Many studies have shown that the after-effects of a sexual assault are extremely distressing and can last a long time. In many cities there are now rape crisis centres where victims can gain both practical and emotional support in coming to terms with the rape and in facing a court appearance.

Sexual offences involving children

Where adults make sexual approaches of any kind towards children, the public react with very strong disapproval. Even if such approaches do not involve any force or violence, the behaviour is considered by the law to be utterly unacceptable. Most sexual approaches towards children do not include intercourse, but take the form of genital touching. The most frequent victims are young girls: a minority of paedophiles are interested in boys.

Why does this sexual interest develop? Some paedophiles find the signs of sexual maturity – pubic hair and enlarged breasts – distasteful. They seek sexual contact with immature females. Other paedophiles may have had a lot of sexual contact with other children during their own childhood, and they have never outgrown this interest. Some paedophiles go the other way. They develop relationships with adult females and then become dissatisfied with them. They feel that the woman is too hard to please, she is too demanding and too unpredictable. They seek the security of a relationship with an undemanding and affectionate child.

The after-effects for the victims seem to be varied. Many show great disturbance and this often lasts through to adulthood. In a few cases, children do not seem to be seriously affected by these experiences, perhaps in cases where the approach was not repeated or forceful. Nevertheless, the law takes the same view of the offence, whether or not force was involved.

Incest

Probably the most common type of offence against children is incest. Because this happens within families, it is likely that many cases go undetected. Reported cases of incest are most commonly between fathers and daughters. The daughters are usually between the ages of ten and fifteen. Incest is not only sexual intercourse, but any attempt to have intercourse with a member of your immediate family. Occasionally women are convicted of incest with their sons; brothers may commit incest with their sisters. It seems that incest is more likely to happen in families where the husband and wife's sexual relationship is unsatisfactory.

Victims of incest often suffer long-term effects. Many women who have been the victims of incest in childhood still experience feelings of guilt and remain afraid of men. They may also have suffered very strained family relationships. Sometimes they feel that they were betrayed by their mothers who did not protect them against the exploitation. They may also feel guilt for sending their father to prison. Often the fact that incest comes to public attention at a trial causes great distress to all family members. If the offender is convicted and sent into custody, then the whole family will suffer the disruption.

In the community there are often self-help groups where victims of incest can share their distress and gain some support from others who have been through the same experience. Women prisoners and young offenders sometimes report that they have been involved in incestuous relationships or that they have been the victims of sexual assault. Where this is reported, it will be helpful if the woman can discuss this in a trusting relationship with a sympathetic listener. Prisoners have time on their hands and they may start thinking about the past. It may be the only opportunity that some of them have to talk about a terrible experience.

Homosexuality

Homosexuality refers to the attraction of a person to a member of the same sex. It can therefore be used for 'gay' men or 'lesbian' women. In the section on sexual development, it was mentioned that our sexual orientation may be influenced from an early age. In adolescence young people often go through a period of exploration or experimentation with members of the same sex but this phase does not last into adulthood. There is another group. Many adult homosexual people report that they were aware of their homosexuality from a very early age. Nobody knows exactly why some people develop homosexual tendencies when the majority of people develop heterosexual attraction (being attracted to the opposite sex). It is probably a complicated mixture of factors including biological features, early experience with other children and later experience with other adolescents, as well as family relationships.

Homosexual activity between consenting males aged twenty-one and over is permitted now in English law. It is still not legally permitted in Scotland, but men are unlikely to be prosecuted for it. It is illegal for anyone under the age of twenty-one. It is also illegal for a man of any age to engage in homosexual activity in a public place, for example, in public lavatories. If they do so, they are liable to be prosecuted.

Some people coming into prison will be homosexual in their orient-ation. This may or may not be connected with their offence. They may be quite sure that this is their sexual identity and be happy with it. Others may come into prison without any previous sexual experience, or they may have been involved with only people of the opposite sex. All these people may develop homosexual tendencies in prison. Because they are contained within an institution and do not have access to their usual sexual partners, they may develop attractions to other prisoners. There are many reports of homosexual activity among women in prison but it is rarely reported for men. This is likely to be because men are much more reluctant to admit it, particularly if they have not been involved in homosexual activity before. It may happen more frequently than we think, particularly where there are two men to a cell.

Whatever the attitude towards homosexual behaviour, it tends to cause problems when it occurs in prison. If the prisoners are both willing partners, it will not distress them, but is likely to disturb staff. One obvious reason for this is that it breaks prison rules. There are other aspects that might concern us, however. It might be that one of the partners is unwilling to engage in the sexual behaviour, but is afraid of the other, and is being forced into doing it under threat. This is more likely where one of the partners is younger, or less experienced in prison and easily frightened. It might happen with both male and female prisoners. In addition, and this seems to happen more often in women prisoners, it is likely that the relationship may develop from a mainly physical one to one involving strong emotion.

Where this happens, there are all the pleasures and pains that occur between lovers, but they are magnified by the closed environment of the prison. It can cause distress to the prisoners and disruption to the prison. It is probably for this reason that the prison rules forbid any activity which might lead to such relationships.

Prostitution

There are various offences associated with prostitution, for example, soliciting, brothel-keeping, living on the earnings of prostitution and procuring. For most of these offences, fines will be imposed, but many people end up in prison for non-payment of fines.

There are many theories to explain why women engage in prostitution. People have said that it is because they have uncontrollable sexual urges, or that they have contempt or hatred for men, or that they have failed to develop into adults and are locked in unhappy childhoods.

There is little evidence to support these ideas, and although psychological factors will influence why a woman enters into prostitution, the economics of the activity seem to be very important. It is a means of earning a regular income and, for some women, it can be extremely lucrative. They obviously hold particular views about sexual behaviour, but their business does not seem to be based on an appetite for sex: it is rarely reported as enjoyable by these women. It is more likely to be an appetite for money, either because of debt, a shortage of cash to pay for necessities, the need to finance drug-taking, or because the women find it the easiest way of getting money. It may also be a behaviour which is learned, or passed on from mother to daughter. In other cases, young teenagers become prostitutes after they have run away from home. Arriving in a big city, with no money and nowhere to stay, they can be easily tempted to try prostitution, and quickly get caught up in the life-style.

Men are also involved in prostitution. They may act either as heterosexual or homosexual prostitutes, or may procure others and earn money that way. They may run considerable organisations that control the practice and income from prostitution.

People have questioned why it is generally only the prostitutes, or those involved in organising or supplying them, who are prosecuted. They have suggested that if there were no customers, there would be no prostitution. In some instances the customers are prosecuted, e.g. in cases of kerb-crawling, or in homosexual prostitution in a public place. But this is much less common than the conviction of the prostitutes themselves.

Sex offenders in prison

Prisoners who have been convicted of sexual offences can cause problems within prison. Just as the press and the public condemn sexual offences, so do other prisoners, particularly where the victims of the offence were very young or very old. Management of such offenders obviously depends on the circumstances of the institution and the regime which it operates but it is often hard for them to be accepted. Segregation into a protected group may solve this problem in the short term but it can have unfortunate consequences. It uses extra resources in maintaining separate accommodation and working conditions. For the prisoner, it means that he is restricted in a small group for a long period of time and this may increase the boredom of imprisonment. It also means that he loses any ability to cope with the taunts of others so that he may never be able to overcome the stigma of his offence.

In some institutions, treatment may be offered either individually or on a group basis. This can take several forms. The offender may be asked to discuss his own family and upbringing in an effort to discover how he developed the behaviour. As mentioned earlier, many sexual offences are expressions of hostility and it may be that the prisoner still has great resentment towards someone who sexually or physically abused him in childhood. Other approaches to treatment use behavioural techniques which aim to discourage the offender's type of sexual behaviour and replace it with some form which is more acceptable to him and society. For example, he may be trained to alter the form of his sexual fantasies away from very young girls, and to start to think about attractive adult women. Further treatment may be offered which is aimed at helping the offender to feel competent in getting on with other people. In that way he will be less inclined to try to show power and dominance by sexual assault.

Any treatment for sexual offences always depends on the offender showing a motivation to change. He has to want to stop offending before any of the techniques can have a chance to work. Unfortunately, not all sex offenders show such motivation and, without it, little can be done to help them.

Within prison, prostitutes are not likely to pose serious management problems. They are often in prison for only short periods. They can require greater attention in terms of health care. They are similar to those offenders who have injected drugs before coming into prison, because there is a risk that they carry serious infections which require either treatment or special management. Infectious hepatitis and HIV (the infection which may lead to AIDS) are the most important of these now.

Summary

This chapter has outlined just some of the sexual behaviour which causes problems for people. It is clear that there are all manner of sexual activities that people practise for different reasons. It is difficult to define what is 'normal' sexual behaviour since there are so many views across the world, and in this country. We have concentrated here on sexual behaviour that causes people problems or breaks the law.

It is important to remember that everyone has their own views about sex. This is why we should hesitate before passing judgement on other people, including prisoners, who end up in custody because of their sexual behaviour.

Chapter four

Alcohol and drugs – their role in criminal behaviour

What is a drug? Ask the man in the street or look at the newspapers. Usually when people talk about drugs they talk about heroin, cannabis, amphetamines or cocaine. 'Record Drugs Haul by Customs Officers', 'M.P.'s daughter in drugs scandal', 'Drugs and AIDS scare'. These headlines bring to our minds images of seedy, rat-infested slums where a group of pale, wasted and dirty individuals share a syringe to inject themselves with some illicit substance or other.

Not all drugs are like these. In medicine, drugs are used to prevent or cure disease. Heroin and amphetamines can have these properties but that is not why they make headlines in the newspapers. What makes a substance a drug which people enjoy using is the effect that it can have on their minds, their feelings or the way they look at things. If we accept this then we have to accept that alcohol, coffee, cigarettes are all drugs just the same as cocaine, cannabis and heroin.

Every day we take into our bodies the food and drink necessary to keep our lives going. We need proteins, fats, sugars, minerals, vitamins and so on. We also take in substances like alcohol, coffee, and nicotine from cigarettes that we do not need physically but which we enjoy or which we feel help us to get through the day. In this chapter we will examine these substances more closely and see how they compare to substances like cannabis and heroin – substances which people usually think of when drugs are mentioned.

Good and bad drugs: good and bad uses

'But heroin and cocaine are hard drugs and even though cannabis is a soft drug it is illegal. How can you compare them to alcohol and cigarettes?'

It is true that these drugs are different because the law sets them apart, but in terms of their effects, it is difficult to draw a dividing line. Looking at the scientific evidence, there is more hard evidence about the harmful effects of tobacco than the harmful effects of cannabis. If we are going to use names like hard and soft drugs, should cigarettes then be thought of as hard drugs?

'What about the illegal drugs? They are addictive, you can get hooked on them.'

A number of the illegal drugs like heroin are addictive, that is, if an individual uses them regularly, he can become physically dependent. If he is deprived of them he feels some effects of that withdrawal. He may also be psychologically dependent on drugs and feel that he needs them to function properly in his everyday life. Both physical and psychological dependence are closely linked and difficult to separate from each other. However, this is also true of the 'legal' drugs. If you have ever tried to give up smoking or to stop drinking tea or coffee you can probably understand what dependence on a drug is like.

'Don't try to tell me I'm a junkie just because I like a drink now and again! I don't go around stoned out of my head, I'm a responsible person and keep within the law.'

Although illicit drugs are similar in some ways to the drugs most people use every day, they become a problem because of how some people use them. Let's look at alcohol as an example. Most people can have one or two drinks socially and leave it at that. Some people find that they have less control over their drinking than others and that can lead them into many more serious difficulties: with their health, their families, their friendships, their work and perhaps also with the law. It is not that alcohol itself in small quantities is bad, the crucial factor is how it is used.

People can experiment with drugs, they can use them occasionally, even quite regularly for pleasure without too many difficulties. It is when drug use reaches the stage where it has an undesirable effect on other aspects of a person's life that it becomes problematic.

Types of drug

Although we are saying that the drug itself is not as important as the way it is used, it is useful to know something about the different effects that various drugs have. The effects are not the same in every person and may vary a good deal according to physical and psychological factors.

A certain dose of drug may have a greater effect on a small person than on someone who is large and heavy. An elderly person or a young child may need less of a drug than a man, someone who expects a particular effect from a drug could need less of the drug to gain that effect than someone with no such beliefs.

Someone whose body is accustomed to regular use of a particular drug may need more and more of that drug to experience the same effects. For example, a teenager unused to drinking may feel and act drunk on two pints of beer, whereas a man who is in the habit of having one or two pints at his local most evenings would require considerably more than two pints to become drunk. This is known as 'tolerance'.

Alcohol

'I had a great night last night; I met Jimmy and Neil and we went down to the pub for a couple of pints. Well, a few actually – what a night! I shouldn't have mixed them though. I felt great last night but this morning . . .'

Most people will be able to understand what this person was feeling; it is a fairly common experience. If we are in any doubt as to the popularity of alcohol in this country we need only to look at the healthy state of the drinks industry. From 1950 to 1976 the amount of alcohol consumed in the United Kingdom increased by 71 per cent according to a World Health Organisation survey.

From prehistoric times, man has drunk alcohol; we know from tomb carvings that the ancient Egyptians did too. We find in the Bible and in the writings of the ancient Greeks and Romans that they all knew the pleasures and problems of alcohol.

In moderation, people find that drinking alcohol helps them to relax and 'let their hair down' a little. Drinking is a sociable thing to do. We drink at the pub, at parties, at dances, with friends – it helps these occasions along. Teenagers and young people may experiment with alcohol as they learn to use it; part of this experience is usually getting drunk, being sick, making fools of themselves, etc. As we begin to understand drink and the quantities that best suit us so that we can feel good without causing ourselves too much discomfort and difficulties; we learn to use it recreationally.

As we are all aware, alcohol can also have its problem side. Let's hear a bit more about the 'morning after the night before'.

'I woke up with my stomach heaving and my head . . . well, I thought it was going to explode. I took one of those pills that the doctor gave my wife for her back, they're really strong painkillers and that made me feel much better. I couldn't eat any breakfast though – all I could take was a couple of cups of black coffee to wake me up and a cigarette to get me going.'

Hangovers are torture at the time but at least they are temporary. Many people have their own favoured remedies: painkillers can help us get over the after-effects. Coffee and cigarettes also give us ways to alter the way we feel. Like alcohol, we can use these other substances to benefit us but they too have the potential for harm.

The effects of alcohol are familiar to most people. Within a few minutes of having a drink, its effects can be felt. These effects vary according to how much alcohol has been taken. A small amount can make you feel more relaxed; emotions such as happiness, sadness, aggression may be expressed more easily. As you drink more you become less inhibited, reacting more emotionally, and you also experience more physical effects – slurring your words, staggering, blurred vision and eventually you may pass out.

If you have ever watched someone getting drunk, you will know that the person himself will often feel and say that he is perfectly in control, whereas it is obvious to you that he is not as capable as he believes himself to be at that time. That is why a great many road accidents involve people who have been drinking.

Heavy drinkers may in the long term suffer from physical problems such as ulcers, liver disease, cancers, heart disease and problems with circulation. If a person drinks to such an extent that he does not eat properly, this, along with liver and stomach problems, can lead to brain damage – in particular, memory problems.

Sometimes alcohol is taken with other drugs which act on the nervous system and the effects of both that drug and the alcohol are exaggerated. When that happens the person will seem more intoxicated or drunk and there may be a danger of overdose.

Tobacco

Tobacco is another drug that acts on the nervous system, which most people recognise. Around 45 per cent of men and 34 per cent of women smoke tobacco in some form although there is some evidence now that more women are taking up smoking than men. Most smokers start in their early teens even though the law forbids the sale of tobacco to those under sixteen.

Nicotine, the main drug in tobacco, has an almost immediate effect which fades quickly. It increases pulse rate and blood pressure and makes you feel stimulated and aroused and is used to help the smoker relax.

The dangers of regular smoking are well advertised: bronchitis, lung cancer, heart disease, etc. Women who smoke in pregnancy are more likely to have smaller babies and run more risk of losing their babies.

Heroin

Heroin is just one of a group of drugs known as the opiates because they come from the opium poppy. Two of the other opiates are codeine and morphine which many people will recognise because of their use in medicine as painkillers. They are also of value in treating coughs and diarrhoea. Heroin, however, is used illicitly because it produces a feeling of relaxation and well-being. These effects can be experienced more rapidly and more intensely if the drug is injected but it is also very often smoked (burnt on tin foil and the fumes inhaled through a cardboard tube); at times it is also 'snorted', that is, sniffed up the nose, rather like snuff.

Pure heroin in moderate doses produces the relaxation and drowsiness the user seeks. If it is used regularly, the dose must be increased to produce the same effects as the system builds up a tolerance to the drug. Whereas this in itself is not life-threatening, a large dose taken by someone unused to it can result in overdose: unconsciousness, breathing difficulties and perhaps death. Frequent use of heroin in the long term can lead to respiratory problems and constipation; menstruation may become irregular or stop altogether. If a woman becomes pregnant while using heroin, the baby may be small at birth and will have withdrawal symptoms which must be treated by experienced medical staff. Users also lose their appetite for food and also for sex; they can be generally apathetic so may be less healthy through not eating properly or taking care of themselves.

The most common health problems amongst heroin users are related not to the drug itself but the way it is used. The black market in heroin is a little like pyramid selling: one dealer will divide what he has, selling it at a profit to other dealers (often themselves users) who repeat the process. To make as much profit as possible, other substances are

31

added to give bulk to the heroin so that, at the end of the line, the person who uses it buys a substance of unknown purity. This can be dangerous if someone who is used to a certain quantity of heroin buys the same amount of a much purer kind without knowing it, as they could overdose themselves. There are also risks with the substances added to the heroin: what the heroin is 'cut' with. This could be anything from chalk to brick dust, from barbiturates to rat poison. They might be harmful in themselves or could cause problems such as infections, blockages, ulcers, and even gangrene if injected. Injecting users can do serious damage to their veins and can develop thrombosis or risk amputation through poor or unclean injecting techniques. There is also the threat of other infections such as AIDS and hepatitis B which are passed on in blood. These infections, however, can only be caught if syringes or other injecting equipment are shared.

If someone who normally uses heroin every day stops suddenly, he will experience some unpleasant withdrawal symptoms; muscular aches, sweating, shivering, watering eyes, sneezing, cramps. Sometimes, some, rather than all, of these are present. They will last a day or two but other symptoms such as sleeplessness could continue for two or three weeks. The user is likely to feel psychologically that he needs heroin to make him feel better.

The other opiates have similar effects and again the problems lie not so much in the drugs themselves but in the way they are used and the life-style of the user.

Amphetamines

The amphetamines are sometimes known to users as 'speed' as this describes their effect; they stimulate the body's systems. Using them (by mouth or injections) can make you feel very energetic, full of ideas, confident and fit. This can last for a few hours and, because of the intense activity that the drug promotes, the user can feel tired and drained afterwards. At high doses, users may have delusions and hallucinations and feel suspicious of people and situations. They may even develop a kind of mental illness or psychosis which may take weeks or even months after stopping amphetamine use to clear. Amphetamines also raise blood pressure and may damage blood vessels and the heart if used often.

There are no great physical problems in ceasing to take amphetamines although people do come to feel that they need them psychologically. A regular amphetamine taker gets used to the stimulating effect of the drug and will use higher and higher doses which may cause the difficulties described above.

Tranquillisers (benzodiazepines)

Apart from alcohol and tobacco, tranquillisers of a type known as benzodiazepines are probably the most widely-used drugs in Britain. They include Valium, Librium, Mogadon, and Ativan which are often prescribed by general practitioners for anxiety, sleeping difficulties or other kinds of emotional upset or stress. They can only be obtained by prescription and it is not an offence to be in possession of them or to give them to someone else. They are also available, illegally, on the black market. They come as pills or capsules and are taken by mouth. Surveys estimate that, in a one-year period, one in seven British adults will have taken tranquillisers, around two-thirds being women. Although doctors have prescribed them less readily in recent years, a large proportion of the population are still given them.

Tranquillisers do what their name implies; they make you feel calm and relaxed and can help sleep. One or two types can go further and make you happy or euphoric. Some of the tranquillisers, particularly at higher doses, cause drowsiness and this can be a danger if driving or operating machinery. If they are taken for more than two or three weeks, their effects (particularly as an aid to sleep) wear off unless the dose is increased. Indeed, if you use tranquillisers as sleeping-pills it may not be helpful in the long run as they can disturb the pattern and balance of your sleep.

Long-term users become highly dependent on these drugs and anxious if they think that a continuing supply may not be available. This dependence motivates them to go on using tranquillisers for a long time after they cease to be of direct benefit. Regular tranquillisers used during pregnancy may cause the baby to have withdrawal symptoms after birth.

It is important to understand that, because of the effects described, 'legal' tranquilliser users can have problems with these drugs as well as the black market users.

Barbiturates

Barbiturates have an effect similar to tranquillisers, giving calmness and sleep. Tuimal and Nembutal are the most commonly misused as they promote a happy 'drunken' feeling. They are less easily available than at one time because since 1985 the law governing their use has been stricter. Now it is illegal to possess them unless they are prescribed to you, and you cannot give them to anyone else. This has meant that barbiturates are also more difficult to obtain on the black market. They cause drowsiness which makes the user more liable to have accidents and may make the person emotional and confused. The long-term user is often susceptible to bronchitis and hypothermia, and babies born to regular users may experience withdrawal symptoms.

Barbiturates can be taken by mouth or injected. Those users who inject are open to the same risks described under the section on heroin which come from poor injecting techniques and unhygienic conditions. Perhaps the greatest danger from barbiturate use is, however, the fact that the amount required to produce an effect is only slightly less than the amount on which a person can overdose. It is very easy then, particularly if you are drowsy and confused, to take too much; you become unconscious and breathing stops.

Cannabis

Originally used as a herbal remedy, cannabis was available on prescription in the UK until 1973. Cannabis is available in different forms, the most common of these being cannabis resin (or the oil extracted from this) and herbal cannabis.

Cannabis resin is compressed and sold in blocks. Herbal cannabis is the direct cannabis plant often known as 'hashish' or 'hash'. These forms are most often smoked, usually combined with tobacco, and they can also be made into a drink or cooked in food. Eating cannabis is the least detectable way of taking cannabis into the body as there is no smoke and no obvious aroma.

Cannabis is probably the most widely used of all the illegal drugs, taken by many people who would not use any other 'street' drug. There is a common belief that cannabis leads people to taking other drugs but there is no evidence to support this and there are many people who have used cannabis exclusively for enjoyment for many years without progressing to any other substance. It is true that a large proportion of, for example, heroin users also take cannabis; they also smoke tobacco yet it would seem ridiculous to suggest that cigarettes were the starting point for a person's heroin-taking.

Like alcohol, the effects of cannabis vary according to the amount taken, the user's mood and the expectations the user has. They begin a few minutes after smoking and last for several hours. To a certain extent, cannabis is an acquired taste in that people generally have to learn to identify its effects on them. People who have used cannabis often describe a feeling of relaxation, talkativeness and enjoyment and greater appreciation of sounds, colours, tastes – in other words, heightened senses. At higher doses, someone can lose their sense of time and think that they see things as bigger or smaller than they really are or their vision may seem distorted. For someone who is unused to using cannabis and who might be feeling upset in some way at the time of use, these effects could be distressing though they do not last.

Research studies of the physical effects of cannabis have produced little evidence of its harmfulness. There is practically no danger of overdose and no withdrawal symptoms. It probably helps to cause breathing problems such as bronchitis and perhaps lung cancer when smoked but this could also be explained by the tobacco which is mixed with it. Anyone suffering from a mental illness might be made worse by the use of cannabis but any symptoms they experience such as confusion or delusions will go after a few days of stopping its use.

Solvents

Over the last ten years or so there has been much concern over young people sniffing glue or other solvents (petrol, aerosols, lighter gas, etc). The effects are rapid due to the solvent itself and to reduced oxygen intake. The user feels 'high' or drunk but if too much is inhaled he can become confused and then unconscious. Most deaths from solvents, however, are not from overdose but from accidents while intoxicated. Long-term heavy use may result in brain damage, particularly with loss of control over movements and kidney and liver problems, but all this is fairly rare. Most difficulties get better when sniffing stops.

Alcohol, drugs and crime

A large number of crimes in Great Britain are associated with alcohol. In particular, a large proportion of violent crimes are committed when the aggressor has been drinking.

Other drugs which have a more relaxing effect tend not to be involved in crime in this way, but as they are illegal and heavy drug use can be expensive, the user may find himself in trouble with the law not only for possession, but also for other crimes which provide the money for his drug use. A number of problem drug users get their drugs by drug-dealing; in selling to others they can hold back a certain quantity for themselves and make enough money to buy a further supply. Others resort to housebreaking, shop-lifting, cheque and credit card fraud, forgery of medical prescriptions and prostitution. It must be said that there are some regular drug-takers who hold regular jobs and pay for their drugs from their earnings.

It has been argued that if the drugs that people choose to take were available to regular users through the National Health Service then there would be much less crime. This plan, however, is not without problems. People generally use drugs to get 'high'; if they take drugs regularly, they need increasing amounts to get 'high' so prescriptions would be for more and more drugs. Drugs on prescription also find their way onto the black market which would make the drug problem worse rather than better. In addition, it might be said that if people can easily get a free supply of drugs, then they have no more incentive to try the difficult process of coming off. The debate still goes on with different groups favouring one option or the other. There seems to be no easy answer.

Coming off drugs

John was first introduced to drugs at a party when he was fifteen years old. A few of his friends had some cannabis; they seemed to be having a good time and suggested he should try it. He agreed. He liked it better than alcohol – and it cost less to get high. He experimented with amphetamines too. When he was around sixteen years old he had the chance to try some heroin; he smoked a bit and after trying it a couple of times he decided that this was what he really liked. For a year or so, whenever he and his friends went to a party or a concert, John would get some heroin as he seemed to enjoy things better with it.

Then things started to go wrong. He had been out with some mates at a party and they decided to nick a car to drive home – it was not the first time they had done it, but this time they crashed the car, and got caught. His dad was furious and threw him out of the house. He went to live with friends but knew that he could not stay there forever. At that time too, his girlfriend found out that she was pregnant. Everything seemed to happen at once. John could not cope with it all. The only thing that helped was the heroin; it made him feel better – the problems were still there but they did not upset him. He relied on it more and more and came to use it daily. Of course, he had to buy the heroin but found that he could get together quite large amounts of money through burglary – videos, televisions and that kind of thing were profitable. He was caught a few times but got away with it more often.

As time went on he had gathered a number of charges and it was inevitable that he eventually received a prison sentence. Three months was not really a long time but what bothered John was coming off the heroin. He had reached the stage where he realised that drugs were making matters worse and wanted to get off. He tried to cut down by himself but that was impossible. Now with a prison sentence, he had the chance to give up. The only worry was how difficult and painful it would be.

He did feel terrible for two or three days, though it seemed longer. He felt as if he had a bad bout of flu – shivering and aching all over. The worst part was not being able to sleep, tossing and turning at night. This took a few weeks to get over but then he began to feel well. Soon he was exercising seriously and managed to get quite fit before his release. He never wanted to go near heroin again.

Although John's physical need for drugs had gone, nothing else had changed. He still had charges outstanding, nowhere to live and problems with his family and his girlfriend. Before too long he was taking heroin again.

John's story is fairly typical of many young drug users who come into the prison system. They can come off drugs when in prison but staying off is the difficulty. It is quite safe for someone suddenly to stop using heroin, even if it is uncomfortable. The same is true for amphetamines. Anyone who has used alcohol or tranquillisers, however, could be at serious risk if they stop taking these suddenly without either reducing gradually or being given some other form of medication. If someone has drunk alcohol heavily and regularly for some time and they suddenly stop, they may sweat, shake and become anxious. They may even become delirious; they are confused and imagine that they are seeing, hearing or feeling things that are not there ('the DTs'). They could, in an extreme case, have fits, become unconscious and die. Certain drugs may be given which reduce these risks. With barbiturates and tranquillisers too, the consequences of sudden withdrawal can be serious. Coming off barbiturates, a person may be irritable and nervous, they have problems sleeping, their limbs twitch and occasionally they may have fits. If they have been using large doses, fits are more likely, they may be delirious and their blood pressure drops very low; without help they may die. It takes about a week for a person to get over these withdrawal symptoms. With tranquillisers it may take about a week for withdrawal symptoms to appear and they may continue for several weeks; some remaining symptoms could go on for months. The person affected may shake and be extremely nervous and anxious, sometimes irritable. They may feel sick and may vomit and if they have been using large amounts they could be confused and have fits.

It is important then that, in the reception process in prisons, efforts are made to identify those who may experience withdrawals early in their stay so that they can be managed appropriately and given medical help if necessary.

Help available

In the community, some doctors and certain hospitals offer people help to come off drugs (to 'detoxify'). Here the user is gradually weaned off his drugs by receiving gradually smaller amounts of a prescribed drug which is the same, or similar to, the drug he has been using; for example, heroin users are normally given reducing doses of a similar drug called methadone which removes some of the unpleasant withdrawal symptoms but gives much less of a 'high' than heroin itself.

To return to John: he found that coming off drugs was much easier than staying off them. This will almost always be the case if the person withdrawing from drugs does not change in themselves or if their situation does not alter. Most people giving up drugs who have been regular users over a long period will need counselling and/or support if they are to be successful.

Within the National Health Service there are a few specialist drug services which can offer that kind of help and there are many other voluntary groups which can provide support of various kinds for drug users. These voluntary groups may be run by users or ex-users, by interested people or may be staffed by professional workers, or a mixture of all three. They may offer counselling, help and advice to users or to their families and friends or may indeed be self-help. They may have fixed meeting times, visit people at home, provide accommodation, offer appointments or operate as a 'drop in' centre. Different kinds of help may suit different people.

Many voluntary groups are quite small organisations which vary from region to region, but it is perhaps worth mentioning one or two organisations that run on a national scale. Most people will be familiar at least with the name of Alcoholics Anonymous. An equivalent group, Narcotics Anonymous, exists for drug users. Both have a similar philosophy – to put it very simply, they believe that addictions are illnesses and the only cure is total abstinence. Once an addict, always an addict; if you give in to your addiction even once you go back to square one, 'one drink, one drunk'. They rely on individual and group support, even pressure at times and are certainly effective for some people. Other agencies would disagree with this 'disease' view, believing that people must accept responsibility for the situations they are in. These groups would try to help the problem drug user or drinker to find alternative activities or interests and learn other ways of controlling their drug use or drinking. In fact, many people nowadays would argue that former problem drinkers can be taught to use alcohol in moderation: being teetotal is not the only choice.

For someone like John, whose life was very much tied up with drugs, it might be necessary to live away from their drug-using or drinking environment. Around the country, there are a number of 'dry' houses, hostels and therapeutic communities which offer people time away from their home situation. In particular, the therapeutic communities provide group therapy so that people can be helped to make changes in themselves as well as in their environment.

It is not only specialist groups and agencies which can help people with drug and alcohol problems but others with some training in counselling: psychologists, psychiatrists, social workers, probation officers and psychiatric nurses may have expertise and experience in this field.

Reducing the risks

There will, of course, be a number of people who are likely to return to their problem drinking and drug-taking after their release from prison. For these individuals it is important that they understand how to reduce as far as possible the harm to themselves. The first thought in most of their minds is to go on a binge as soon as they are released. This is the first danger. As we have learned, most drugs and alcohol in large quantities can be harmful to those who are not used to them. What people do not realise is that when they have not had a particular drug or alcohol for some time, their bodies get used to doing without it and are unable to take as much of that drug or alcohol as they once did. It is fairly common for individuals not to think of this when coming out of prison, to take too much and to overdose.

The second main area where harm can be minimised is for injecting drug users. We have already thought about their problems and it is clear that a number of risks lie in the injecting itself. Using clean needles and syringes ('works') can help a great deal. These can be bought at a number of pharmacists and, in many areas of the country, there are exchange schemes where dirty needles and syringes can be swapped, free of charge, for clean ones.

Alcohol and drug use in prison staff

It is important to remember that problem drinkers and drug users can come from all walks of life and all occupations. People in high-stress jobs may turn to alcohol and drugs to help them to cope. As the prison officer's work is stressful at times, he or she may be vulnerable to such problems. As we have mentioned before, alcohol and prescribed drugs such as tranquillisers can lead to just as many problems as illegal ones. It is also much easier to deal with difficulties as they arise before they get out of hand. It may be difficult to talk to colleagues or senior officers about any problems but your general practitioner may be able to help you find someone to talk to in confidence, or a local voluntary alcohol/drug group may help in this way.

Summary

Broadly speaking, drugs are substances which can alter your psychological state. That is, they can affect your mood, your thinking and your perception of things. Almost every drug that exists can be helpful or harmful depending on how it is used.

If someone is a problem drug user, they are not properly controlling their use of a particular drug (or drugs). This is leading them into difficulties with their health, with their relationships with other people, with their work or with the law. Many crimes are committed either under the influence of drugs or alcohol or in order to support an individual's drinking or drug use.

Drugs, including alcohol, can be very difficult to give up. Many drugs have physical effects on the body which leave someone with unpleasant symptoms when they stop taking the drug. These vary from drug to drug but some withdrawal symptoms can be distressing and, at times, life-threatening. Even if a person is not physically dependent on a particular drug, he or she can have cravings for it which are difficult to resist, in spite of how much they might want to give up their drug use.

There is also a specific danger for someone being released from prison being free of drugs. If they go back to drug use, they could easily overdose as their bodies are not able to take as much of that drug as they did while using it regularly.

There are many agencies, voluntary and in the health and social services, which provide a service to drug users. They can offer help and advice both to prisoners and ex-prisoners and to officers who may turn to drug use of any kind as a result of work stresses.

Chapter five

Understanding violence and aggression

'Youth dies in gang-fight stabbing', 'Battered wives speak out; the truth about growing family violence', '17 injured in car-bomb blast', 'Granny-bashers strike again; 78-year-old woman mugged at home', 'Prison officer in hostage roof-top drama', 'Man shot in betting-shop raid', 'Child-abuse on the increase'.

Open a newspaper any day of the week and there will be headlines like these. People say we are living in a violent society. Many have ideas about what can be done to improve the situation. It seems, however, that we cannot make useful plans for change until we understand some of the causes of aggression and violence. The question of how people come to act in this way is the theme of this chapter.

Key words

The words 'violence' and 'aggression' are often used loosely. In this book we use 'violence' to mean a physical attack: fighting, punching, kicking, using a weapon. 'Aggression' has a more general meaning, not just physical assaults. It can refer to verbal attacks (argument, destructive criticism, sarcasm, name-calling) or even just a hostile attitude.

Physical violence is clearly our main interest when we talk about criminal behaviour; nevertheless, violence may begin with a hostile approach or a verbal row and so it is necessary to pay attention to these types of aggression also.

Kinds of aggression

Criminal aggression and violence differ from the sort of aggression that most people experience in everyday life. Most people never reach the stage when they are so angry that they could injure another person. Despite this, the nature of criminal and 'normal' aggression is the same. The causes and the feelings involved are similar: criminal violence is merely a more extreme expression of them.

If we are trying to understand criminal aggression, a good point to start might be to look at 'normal' aggression. We may never have hit anyone but there are few people who can say that they have never lost their temper or spoken angry words. When people describe their own experiences of aggression they will use expressions like 'I just blew up', 'I lost my head', 'I flew off the handle'. They may even talk about losing control or not thinking about what they were doing. Without doubt, anger can be a very strong emotion which can cause us to act in ways which we might later regret. However, feelings of anger may not be the only reason why people act aggressively.

Imagine the situation in a prison wing; for the last three days one of the prisoners has been five or ten minutes late for his work-party. The principal officer tells him firmly to be more careful about his time-keeping. The next day the prisoner is late again and this time the principal officer is angry with him and warns him in no uncertain terms to be on time tomorrow. The principal officer was angry but he also chose to express his anger in order to try to make a point to the prisoner. He used anger to make the prisoner change his behaviour.

This kind of aggression may be seen in everyday working life. It is noticeable where there are clear rules to follow and staff have ranks or definite positions of authority. The discipline side of the prison service is one example of this sort of situation. Where the lines of management are less clear it becomes more difficult to be aggressive, especially with colleagues and friends at approximately the same rank.

Most people at some time will have had cause to telephone a large organisation. You may have been enquiring about your income tax, or querying an electricity bill. Whatever the circumstances, it is not uncommon for someone to be passed from one department to another. You have to explain your problem each time and become more and more frustrated. In the end, it seems that the only way to get anywhere is to shout down the telephone and demand to speak to the person in charge. In other words, aggression can be used for a purpose.

Learning aggression with a purpose

From an early age we learn to use aggression to get what we want. A two-year-old child is being wheeled round the supermarket in a trolley. He notices his favourite chocolates on a shelf just within his reach. He helps himself to a large packet. His mother says 'No, you had sweets in the car on the way here', she takes them out of the trolley and puts them back. He picks them up again. 'No', his mother says, 'they're bad for your teeth', and so it goes on. He begins to cry and then shout. His voice rises to a scream and he kicks furiously against the side of the trolley. Other shoppers turn round and stare, his mother becomes increasingly embarrassed and in the end gives in. The tantrum stops.

The same boy, Peter, is now three years old and goes to play-group. One of the favourite games there is to make guns from Lego bricks and play at having battles. Unfortunately, there are only a few long bricks suitable for making guns. One morning he arrives early and to his joy finds a long brick and makes a gun. A short time later, Sam arrives; he is almost five years old. He wants to join in the battle which his friends are having. He sees the gun in Peter's hand and grabs it off him. Peter goes after him and struggles to get the gun back but Sam hits him with it. Peter begins to cry and has to find another toy to play with.

When Peter has been at the play-group longer, he finds that he too can get the toys he wants in this way. As he grows up he learns more about how to use aggression in playground fights, verbal and physical. He might, for example, find that, for him, calling other children names might be more effective in helping him get what he wants. In his teenage years perhaps, he discovers that mockery and more subtle sarcasm can be quite intimidating, even to adults. All the time he learns ways of being aggressive which can get results.

Most people learn to achieve what they want by a variety of means; persuasion, humour, charm, etc. We know how to be aggressive but choose to use this more or less, depending on what kind of person we are and what other skills we have in dealing with situations.

People may act aggressively, then, for two main reasons: (1) because of angry feelings, or (2) as a means of getting what they want. These two things are usually not entirely separate. Considering all the violent crimes that take place, few are only for gain, financial or otherwise. In this category may be violent bank robberies, perhaps some kidnappings, only if they are carried out in what might be described as a cold-blooded way. By way of contrast there are many violent acts committed in a fit of blind rage, such as 'crimes of passion'. Most aggressive actions involve some element of gain; of money, status, publicity, etc, and some element of emotion; anger, frustration, or jealousy.

Gains from aggression

In the sort of aggression we have just been discussing, aggression with a purpose, it can be very clear what a person stands to gain by acting in this way. Young Peter may have learnt how to get a toy, the bank-robber may run off with the loot, the mugger gets his victim's wallet.

Sometimes the gains from violence might not be obvious. A husband and wife disagree, he hits her and she gives in: so next time there is a difference of opinion, he knows how to get his own way. Of course, feelings may be involved but the fact that being aggressive gets results can be enough for that kind of behaviour to be repeated. Very often it becomes an easier way to settle disputes than the hard business of negotiation.

A group of youths may be feeling aggressive for many different reasons, but gang fights will develop largely to build up reputations for those involved. Here the pay-off for being violent is the status of being known as a 'hard man'.

Even less clear are those instances of aggression occurring most commonly with children and people with a mental handicap who injure either themselves or others. Here their motivation seems to be to attract attention to themselves, even if that attention is quite negative, perhaps even involving some form of punishment.

It must be emphasised that although the kind of aggression we have described does have a purpose, the individual concerned may not make a conscious decision to behave in that way. As has been suggested, he may have learned over the years to use violence and it may seem more obvious to him to act aggressively rather than to find other ways of getting his own way.

We have already explained that aggressive behaviour may also come about because of how someone feels. It is this aspect of aggression that we shall now consider.

What makes people aggressive?

People may feel annoyed and end up by acting aggressively in response to things and people around them and also to their own physical and mental states. In this section each of these factors will be discussed in turn. They will be described in four different parts:

1) what a person feels like inside (physically and mentally),
2) the degree of discomfort in the surroundings,

3) the behaviour of others,
4) personal thoughts.

Internal feelings

Since starting to work in this field, we have asked a number of people who do not have a problem with aggression to tell us about the last time they felt angry.

It is an interesting exercise to do for yourself. Think back to the last incident you can remember; it does not need to have been very striking or dramatic. Try to write down when it happened, where, if anything relevant had occurred just before, what actually went on and how you responded to the situation. It might be useful to keep this record by you to refer to while you read the rest of this chapter. You could find that some of the points which will be discussed may mean more to you if you can relate them to your own experience.

Very often, when people have done this exercise, we have heard them start out with some sort of description of how they felt at the time. For example, Paul is a nurse on a unit where staff who normally work days have to do periods of night duty for two to three weeks. He does not particularly like working nights because it normally takes him a week or so to get used to sleeping during the day. He describes the background to the aggressive incident he has recorded. He writes:

> It was over the holiday period and there were problems with finding enough cover for the ward at night. I needed the extra money and agreed to do five nights in a row. My car was due for its MOT so I was spending quite a few hours during the day working on that. I just felt shattered.

Tiredness is a common state which people say makes them prone to aggression. Pain, especially something like a toothache, and hunger can also make people more irritable than usual.

Another way of altering your internal state is through drink or drugs. Alcohol is frequently associated with violence because of two of its main effects. First, those who have ever seen someone who is drunk or, indeed, have themselves drunk alcohol in large amounts will testify that alcohol can have a dramatic effect on a person's mood. There are the caricatures of the happy drunk singing his way home, reeling along cheerily and talking to everyone on the way. There is the morose drunk, crying into his beer. And, of course, there is the fighting drunk picking arguments with anyone around. Not only does alcohol make people feel different, perhaps more aggressive, it exaggerates that mood; it becomes larger than life.

The second effect of alcohol is not so much to do with how a person feels as how he or she controls the expression of that feeling. Individuals who under normal circumstances are quite reserved and not demonstrative may try to hug and kiss others when under the influence of alcohol. The things which usually hold us back from acting on our feelings do not function or are ignored.

Certain drugs, like alcohol, may alter mood and make people less inhibited about their behaviour. But it is much less common for other drugs to be implicated in violent incidents. Caffeine, which is contained in coffee, tea, chocolate, cocoa, cola drinks and Iron Bru, is known to make people more irritable when taken in moderately large amounts. In addition to this, there is an increasing interest in research into food allergies which suggests that certain individuals who act aggressively may in fact be especially sensitive to particular things in their diet, such as refined sugar.

Apart from drink, drugs and some foods, other factors can influence the likelihood of someone acting aggressively. Clearly, if a person is experiencing psychological difficulty, he may have less control over his temper.

Frank is 56 years old and has just been made redundant for the second time. He is married to Cathy and they have two daughters and one son, all of whom have their own homes now. They have few financial worries as Frank was given redundancy pay and Cathy has a secretarial job. Over the last few weeks he has become more and more despondent and low in mood. He has trouble sleeping and has lost interest in going out to visit friends which he had always enjoyed. When his wife has tried to help he snaps at her which results in terrible rows.

In Frank's case, he is probably suffering from depression, one of the symptoms of which can be irritability. Most of us never become depressed to the extent where we would be considered to be mentally ill; nevertheless, we all have times where we feel sad or low in spirits. At such times we may take things more seriously than we need; maybe we act more impulsively and this frequently emerges as aggression. This is also true of the times when we are worried or anxious.

When individuals describe their own aggressiveness, they often talk about responses to fairly trivial incidents: a major row developing out of, for instance, the cap being left off the toothpaste. This is what you might call 'making a mountain out of a molehill'. However, when you question that individual more closely, that trivial happening is invariably the last of a series of perhaps small, but irritating, events. Each event serves to make that person feel more and more tense. As that tension increases, so does the likelihood of an aggressive reaction to an apparently minor incident.

We have now considered those factors inside ourselves, both mental and physical, which contribute to aggressive feelings and actions. Now let us look for a while at some of the things which impinge on us from outside.

Discomfort in the surroundings

Think of a busy town road at 5.15 in the afternoon. There has been a crash up ahead and the queue of traffic has slowed down and then ground to a halt. It is November, pouring with rain and quite chilly. A few horns sound but everyone huddles in their cars feeling miserable as their windows mist up.

Now think about the same incident, this time in June. It is the middle of a freak British heat-wave. Inside the cars it is hot and sticky. Car horns blow, drivers already have their windows open to try to keep the car cool. Motorists put their heads out of the windows and start to shout at each other. Tempers are hot, like the weather.

Nowadays we often hear about noise pollution. Can this, like the temperature, affect our tempers? It has become so common to hear parents talking about the volume of their teenage children's pop music that it is now part of the stereotype of the parent–teenager generation gap. With younger children also, it is hard to imagine a scene of a harassed young mother shouting at her offspring without including noise. The baby crying, the six-year-old running around pretending to be He-man and launching himself off the chairs with loud shrieks. Most of us would find it hard to keep calm if a man with a pneumatic drill were digging up the road outside our house on a Sunday morning. Prisoners who cannot escape from the hubbub of a normal jail can feel more aggressive because of the noise level.

Temperature and noise have been mentioned specifically, but other elements in the environment which have an unpleasant effect on any of our senses might arouse aggressive responses in us. Different individuals will no doubt be sensitive to different things; for example, fluorescent lights, itchy clothing, the smell of paint or petrol. If something in our environment makes us feel uncomfortable it can cause tension, and one effect may be to make us feel and act more aggressively.

In prisons the environment is unlikely to help inmates to be calm and non-violent. Rooms are often too hot or too cold; they are small and usually without sanitation so they are liable to smell. During summer nights they are light which may make it difficult for some inmates to sleep easily. There is frequently the noise of people moving around or banging on pipes. This, of course, does not apply to all establishments, but consider a prison you know and try to think of the things about its environment which would irritate you if you had to live there.

The behaviour of others

Why does a person who feels aggressive act on that feeling in one situation but not in another? One possible answer to this question is that it depends on how others act towards him.

We hear reports of the 'escalation' of violence in South Africa or Northern Ireland or in the Lebanon. Basically what that means is that one side brings in even bigger guns or more powerful long-range missiles or more troops or better rubber bullets. Naturally, the other side does not want to lose, so it buys new weapons or recruits more soldiers to match its opponent's increased strength. So the conflict rises, as on an escalator, and like an escalator, it is very difficult to stop it going up. As the pattern is repeated, more extreme violence is unavoidable.

Most of us, thankfully, are not involved in world conflict, but the same sort of process occurs on a smaller scale between individuals. If a person is behaving aggressively and disagrees with another, whether this situation is resolved or whether it ends in violence may depend on how that second person reacts.

Picture a crowded pub on a Saturday night. People have been drinking for an hour or so but no one is obviously drunk. Dave squeezes through the crowd to the bar and buys three drinks. When the barman is getting his order other people clamour for service behind him. He turns around to carry the drinks back to where his friends are sitting but the man standing next to him accidentally jogs his arm. Most of the drink Dave was carrying in his left hand is spilt.

Let us examine some possible outcomes of this situation. It may be that the two settle this problem in a friendly way, as follows.

Man: Oh, sorry pal. It was an accident, I'll get you another.
Dave: That's fair enough, thanks.

Clearly, if the man had ignored that accident this could have aroused ill-feeling. The way that Dave might have responded is also important. For example,

Man: Oh, sorry pal. It was an accident, I'll get you another.
Dave: I should think so too. Why don't you look where you're going? You're so desperate to get a drink, you just shove everyone else out of the way.

By acting in this way Dave is likely not only to lose the opportunity to have another drink bought for him, but also to make the man angry. Using aggression tends to promote further aggression.

Many people for whom aggression is a problem may act in this kind of way. That is, they respond angrily even when the person they are dealing with is acting in a reasonable way. There is also a second type of person whose aggressive behaviour develops from the way they handle others. This is the sort of person who will go along with other people's ideas and requests without disagreeing. Although they may feel that they do not want to do a particular thing, or are opposed to a certain opinion, they say nothing. Their feelings of annoyance and irritation build up the more they are put upon and this ultimately results in a sudden, aggressive outburst.

In both cases, the individual requires to learn to deal with others in a more appropriate way. He/she needs to develop skills in expressing opinions in a clear and direct way without being rude to the other person, and needs to allow the other person to express a point of view. In Chapter 8 we look at how you can be assertive – get your point across – without resorting to aggression. Being assertive is a skill involving words and body language: not just what someone says, but how they say it – the impression they give others by the way they stand, the expression on their face, their gestures and so on.

Dealing with other people is an art. Like other arts, it needs to be practised. We teach children to say 'please' and 'thank you' but any parent will testify that they have to be told many times to do so. Children, for their part, must repeat 'please' and 'thank you' many times, in many different situations before it comes naturally. We are not born to say these words but look at adults in a shop, at work, at a party. Most adults will use some form of these words (thanks, ta, cheers, etc.)

when asking for something, or when they are handed something. This kind of learning, therefore, must be effective.

This does not mean that the answer lies in teaching manners to violent offenders! It implies only that handling people in the right way does not always come naturally to people. Most of us have to learn something about it. Much of this we are taught or absorb by observation when we are children or teenagers. As adults we might find that the way we have been treating others is not always helpful. New skills can be learned, given a little time and help. It might seem more difficult because we have to unlearn bad habits and we feel more self-conscious about it, but it can work.

Different skills may be more or less useful to different people. For example, a couple have domestic arguments which normally result in the wife being battered and the husband feeling guilty about it. It might help them considerably to learn to listen to each other without jumping to conclusions about what the other is thinking. Negotiating and compromise would also be helpful strategies for them. Similarly, a young lad with a record for police assault and violence against those in authority may need to learn to accept reasonable orders and give criticism in a less dangerous way.

The third main component, then, in violence and aggression is the way a person deals with others and how they behave towards him.

Personal thoughts

Having discussed how we act and how others act towards us, it is necessary to go on to consider thoughts. Thoughts and behaviour are closely linked.

When we look at other people, we assume a great deal about them; sometimes our ideas may be accurate, sometimes not. There is a television advert that illustrates this well. A teenage boy stands at a street corner, his head is shaven, he wears heavy boots, jeans and a denim waistcoat. His clothes are hung with chains and safety pins. You think 'This is a young thug, hanging around, looking for trouble'. A car pulls up and he runs away. You think 'Ah, the police have come to pick him up. He is guilty and trying to escape'. Then you see him running away from the camera, towards a well-dressed, oldish man with a bowler hat. The man holds his brief-case up in front of him as the lad lunges towards him. You think 'The man looks wealthy and would be an easy target. The youth is going to mug him'. The final shot is from further off so that the viewer can see the whole scene. You notice that there is scaffolding around one of the buildings in the street and the workmen are hoisting up a pallet of bricks. The lad standing at the corner notices that the pallet is tipping and will fall on the man beneath and so runs to pull the man out of the way.

The picture we have of other people is usually incomplete. We make assumptions about what another person is like, what mood they are in and how they might react. We behave according to our assessment of them. As we continue to be with that other person and converse with them, we can gather more information about them. If our thoughts about them are flexible, we can alter our ideas according to this new knowledge. The more accurate our guesses about the other person, the better we can be in dealing with them appropriately. However, if our thoughts are very rigid and we stick by our original opinion, we could end up by dealing with that other person in a very clumsy way.

John is walking down the street; he notices Peter coming towards him. John smiles and nods at him from a distance. Peter looks at him but makes no sign of recognition. John thinks 'He's ignoring me. I'm not going to let him get away with that'. As Peter gets closer, he is about to walk past but John stops him. Peter says that he didn't see him. John thinks 'He's just making excuses; he's trying to avoid paying the £3 he owes me'. He talks to Peter, but receives only very brief answers. Peter is looking round, obviously wanting to go. John thinks 'He's trying to get away'. He says to him 'Do you have that money you owe me?' Peter looks blank. John gets annoyed and begins to get aggressive. Peter says that there was no need for him to act in that way and an argument follows.

John might have acted differently if he had known that Peter's girlfriend had that day been rushed into hospital. He was on his way there to find out how she was and was so preoccupied that he did not notice John in the street nor was he concentrating on their conversation. Perhaps John could not have known this at the beginning of their meeting, but if he had not acted solely on his first thoughts he might have given his friend a chance to tell him. By behaving as though he thought that Peter was trying to dodge him and avoid his debt, what John said and the way that he said it would be hostile. In such an exchange, the other person would be unlikely to talk easily about his worries.

Some individuals who are inclined to act violently say that fights may start if someone even looks at them 'the wrong way'. This normally means that they suppose, without any other evidence, that the other person is criticising or looking down on them. Aggression may occur therefore if someone misinterprets what he sees or hears. Anger may also arise if an individual reads too much into the information they have.

For example, Julia is away on business for a week and she has arranged to phone her boyfriend, Mark, on Wednesday early in the evening. By 11 p.m. she still has not called. He thinks 'She must be out with someone else. She will be enjoying herself too much with him to think of me. She will never get in touch with me again now. The bitch! I won't let her use me like that'. Mark's ideas could be true but it might be more reasonable not to make an immediate judgement but to find out what happens when Julia does get in contact. She may have had a business dinner. It may have been necessary to complete some urgent work that evening. She could have been so tired that she fell asleep in the evening and did not wake until it was too late to phone. By exploring other explanations, angry feelings may be allayed.

The other factor which makes aggression more likely is when a person feels that he or she is under attack. In the example above, Mark may have thought that Julia was being unfair or unreliable, but perhaps more importantly he also felt it was a blow to his self-respect. It is easier for us to become aware of these kinds of thoughts about ourselves with practice. Mark may not have been entirely conscious of it, but the reason he reacted so dramatically could have been that he felt that Julia's silence was a kind of criticism of him. His thoughts may have been, 'Julia does not care enough about me even to phone. She has probably found someone better than me. I am not good enough. I should be more attractive'. The less self-respect a person has, the more difficult it is for him or her to brush off what seems to be a criticism. If an individual feels him or herself to be criticised, they defend themselves, often aggressively.

A person's thoughts, both about him or herself and about others, can be a powerful influence on his or her reactions to situations and the chances of aggression occurring.

Summary

Criminal aggression is more exaggerated than the aggression most people experience in everyday life. Nevertheless, its causes may be similar to those which make most of us feel or behave aggressively. Aggression can be learned early in our childhood years and used throughout our lives not only to express anger and frustration but also as a means of getting our own way. If an individual gains from acting aggressively, he will do so again and this behaviour will continue unless he finds that it is no longer advantageous.

People may feel angry and frustrated if they are uncomfortable physically (tired, hungry, in pain) and mentally (worried, depressed). Aggression and violence may occur if an individual is in an unpleasant environment (if it is too hot, if it is excessively noisy). If someone acts in a hostile way they are likely to get a hostile response. An individual who is not skilled in dealing with other people may provoke aggression in others and react aggressively himself.

A person is more likely to be aggressive if they assume that another individual is being hostile to them. This may be a mistaken assumption if they fail to allow their ideas to be modified according to the evidence available. Someone who has little confidence in themselves may be sensitive to criticism or may think that criticism is implied when it is not. These individuals may feel the need to defend themselves and may do so in an aggressive way.

Chapter six

Psychological disturbance in prison

When we work in prisons we tend to take them for granted. We get blasé about what being in prison does to prisoners. We see prisoners behaving in an unusual fashion and we don't really try to work out why. We explain it in slogans: 'he can't do his time', 'he should get his head down and get on with his sentence'. In this chapter we will look at the psychological effects of being in a prison. By understanding some of the difficulties that prisoners face we can help them get through their sentence. If you can do that it makes prison life easier for prisoners, but it also makes it easier for everyone who works in prisons. Prisoners don't just have the pressures of being in prison to cope with but they may have to cope with problems which are happening outside the prison. A wife might have an affair, a son may get into trouble with the police, a father may contract a terminal illness or a daughter may start using heroin. All these problems would cause difficulties in any family. Being inside prison makes them even harder to cope with. Let us consider some of the problems of being a prisoner and what effects they can have.

Loss of control

Most of us enjoy living a free life. We develop likes and dislikes about the sort of food that we prefer, the cars we like, our friends, our clothes and the places we like to go on holiday. We also enjoy choosing the things we like, and can become annoyed if we have to put up with things or people that we dislike. The ability to choose how we live our lives is very important to us. When someone comes into prison, this ability to choose is taken away. Prisoners cannot even choose when to do the most basic human functions, like washing, dressing, going to the toilet, going to sleep, or choosing when or what to eat. All these very ordinary, but very important behaviours are outside the prisoner's control. Although we go through this experience in childhood, it comes as quite a shock to an adult to lose control of life in this way. It can lead to all kinds of reactions: anger, frustration, bewilderment, agitation, feelings of hopelessness or depression. Many prisoners find it humiliating and frightening, particularly the first time that it happens.

Loss of family

One of the most obvious changes that takes place coming into prison is that the prisoner leaves behind family and friends. Often these are the only people in whom the prisoner can confide. One of the best ways of handling pressure is to talk to someone who will listen and understand. Most people confide in their family; if they are not available, the pressure just goes on building up.

For families outside, the change can be just as upsetting. It is particularly difficult where there are children in the family. Prisoners often worry about what to tell the children. This adds to the pressure. Is it better to tell the truth and take the risk that children will be teased at school? Or should the family have a story about the mother or father being away working or in a hospital? There is no right or wrong answer to this problem: it is up to the individual prisoner to decide what to do. It seems, however, that children often guess where the parent is, and are less distressed than everyone anticipates. If they do guess, then the prisoner should be open with the child and give reassurance that he or she has not left forever.

Separation from those whom we love is usually painful. If there is the possibility of communication, this helps to ease the situation. Letter-writing, which is the main means of communication from within prison, does not necessarily come that easily to all prisoners. It also involves a delay, so that questions and problems that arise do not get an instant response from the person on the receiving end. Sometimes this is a good thing. It means that both parties have time to think about what they say to each other and serious arguments can be avoided. At other times this delay can have drawbacks. A prisoner who has heard a rumour, or been told of something that has happened outside prison, may have to wait days before having it confirmed or denied. It is important to realise how much prisoners depend on letters.

In prisons where telephones are available to prisoners, there are other problems of communication with the outside world. There is no delay, so things can be said on the spur of the moment and later regretted. A prisoner may then have to wait for the next opportunity to phone before trying to put things right again.

The effects of a parent's imprisonment on the child have not been thoroughly studied. There is, however, quite a bit of research on the effects of separation for other reasons. Much depends on the child's relationship with the parent beforehand. Even in cases where the relationship was not particularly good, a young child is likely to be confused and distressed by separation. They may go through a period of protesting, being angry about what has happened. Later they may become more withdrawn and seem to ignore the prisoner parent. This is a worrying reaction for the prisoner, but it may help to know that it is a stage that children often go through after separation, and that the child may settle to accept the situation later. Acceptance of the situation is made easier if children are given reassurance. The parents can show that they still care for the child even though they have had to go away.

Visiting obviously helps families to keep in touch but there are some difficulties associated with visits. One of the frustrations for prisoners is the short length of visits, particularly after a long period of separation. It means that all the thoughts and ideas that have been occurring over the past weeks have to be condensed into a short period of conversation. If an argument occurs or the conversation gets side-tracked onto a different issue, then important things may be left unsaid.

Another frustration is that if the visits are closed, then there is not only a barrier to touching visitors, but a hindrance to the conversation because hearing what the other person has to say is more difficult. These factors add a strain to the visit. Although these may sound relatively trivial matters, to the prisoner they become all-important. The visit is the highlight of the time in prison and it assumes enormous importance. Children may also find the situation frustrating, particularly when they do not understand the circumstances. For these reasons, some prisoners decide that they would rather not put their children through the experience. This is why some prisoners do not arrange passes for their children to visit.

Apart from visits, contact with children can be maintained by letter. If children are not able to write, they can send drawings they have done. It is important for those in prison to remain involved in the welfare of their children. Those outside who are left caring for the children will appreciate any support that the prisoner can give. This means that if the child is having difficulty at school, or is behaving badly at home, the prisoner can be a help merely by listening to the problems, even if he or she does not know the answer. The prisoner may feel powerless to help and the person caring for the child outside may not think that the prisoner can help, but it is still important to be involved. Otherwise the prisoner becomes out of touch with the child's development. This may create problems after release.

Keeping in touch with the child's development is just as important for babies as it is for older children. Many fathers who are in prison when their babies are born can be distressed by the fact that they are so far away, and cannot be of help at the time of the birth. It is important that they do see their babies as soon as possible so that they are included in the family. For women whose babies are born while they are serving a prison sentence, the importance of an early bond has been recognised. In many prisons women can keep their young infants with them, up till the age of about eighteen months. Efforts ought to be made to try to keep families of prisoners in touch as much as possible. One way of coping with the stress of separation that prisoners experience is often to cut off feeling and emotion. While this may help the prisoner to cope with the sentence, in the long term it is damaging to relationships within families. It has often been said that in punishing the offender, by sending him or her to prison, we are also punishing the family. Prisoners and their families should try to minimise the damage that is done to family relationships.

Lack of stimulation

Apart from missing family and friends, the prisoner also misses other kinds of day-to-day activity. The routine of prison and the fact that there is little variety in the surroundings, in the faces that you see and in the work that you do, means that life can become monotonous. This lack of stimulation can affect the way that people think. In a number of studies on the effects that lack of stimulation can have, it seems that the ability to think is altered. It becomes harder to solve problems. Although the general level of intelligence is not affected, people find it difficult to work out the solutions to tasks that they have to do. This is something that happens to people who are kept in restricted environments, whether it is a submarine, a prisoner-of-war camp, a concentration camp or as a lone sailor on an ocean-going yacht.

One way to combat this effect is to try to control the environment in some way: to make the most out of the very limited opportunities. This has been reported by prisoners-of-war. They may work out systems of communication to pass messages to others, or make things out of pieces of twig, or metal, or try to persuade their guards to get things for them. In other situations, people may invent games or rules for themselves about what they must do with their time: twenty press-ups before breakfast, or a page of the diary before lunch etc. Prisoners may do this sort of thing for the same reason. They may develop special habits which they must keep up, or they may try to manipulate others so that they can have some control over their unusual environment. This can cause difficulties for management. Such behaviour may well increase with lack of stimulation. If a prisoner is kept in isolation, out of circulation, he may try to exert control even more. If prisoners have the opportunity to control their environment in a useful way, by choosing which hall they are in or which activities they engage in, they are less likely to try to exert control in ways which disrupt the running of the institution. Isolation can have strange effects on even the strongest prisoners. One prisoner who served several years in effective solitary confinement described how he slipped in and out of madness; his thoughts became odd, he lost track of where he was, time became distorted. He became more dangerous. He was frightened to come out of his cell and over-reacted when people invaded his territory by coming into his cell.

One of the fears that long-term prisoners have is that they will lose their intelligence while in prison. They are already aware that they will be quite a bit older when they get out of prison. They may also think that they will be unable to cope with the intellectual demands of life. As mentioned earlier, there is no evidence that general intellectual ability is damaged by imprisonment, but it does appear that problem-solving is affected. These are effects of 'institutionalisation' and are common to many people who have spent periods of time in large institutions, e.g., prisons or hospitals. Many of the effects that have been mentioned so far are effects that happen when people are grouped together and have choices removed from them. The ability to choose, if not practised, becomes more difficult to use.

Loss of models

For young offenders who come into prison, there are other important changes. They are still at a stage of development where they imitate others. Outside in the community, they may copy their friends, parents, older brothers or sisters. Inside prison there are fewer models to copy – there are only other young offenders. This means that they are easily influenced by the more sophisticated inmates who often attempt to exploit the situation. In the short term, this creates management problems. In the long term, it affects the way that the young offender will develop. There is some truth in the idea that prisons are 'schools of crime'. Young offenders are likely to want to copy the more notorious young offenders and may become more involved in crime.

Psychological disturbance

So far the general effects of imprisonment have been described. Sometimes the psychological disturbance is such that it causes the prisoner considerable distress. This may not be immediately obvious, because the distress may not appear as a 'psychiatric disorder' but erupts in anger, violence, self-injury or withdrawal. For this reason, the commonest forms of psychological disorder, anxiety and depression, will be described here.

Anxiety

Everyone experiences anxiety at some time or other. It is part of normal human existence. We feel anxious before interviews, when we have to give public talks, or if we know that we have to face a difficult situation with someone. Anxiety can show itself in all kinds of ways: you may feel your heart pounding, your mouth may become dry, your face or hands may sweat, you may have blurred vision, dizziness, a choking feeling, pains in the head, neck, shoulders or stomach, feel sick or faint, or experience many other symptoms.

Think back to the last occasion when you were anxious and try to remember how you felt. Your pattern of anxiety is likely to be different from your friend's or colleague's. Sometimes there is a feeling that you are not really here, or that things around you are not real. This can be very frightening and can make the anxiety worse.

For many people anxiety like that happens just before important occasions, but they do not suffer it all the time. But for others, particularly if they are under stress through work or personal difficulties, the anxiety can become constant. They may begin to feel some of these symptoms every day.

There are various ways of coping with anxiety like this. If you live outside prison you may confide in a friend or relative and try to relieve your worries that way. You may go and do something – paint a room, play football or go out for a drive – to take your mind off the thoughts that are making you anxious. If things get really bad you might go to your family doctor to talk things over: sometimes doctors prescribe medication to lessen the symptoms. Some people turn to drink, in the hope that it will wipe out the feelings (although it frequently makes them worse).

If you are a prisoner and you suffer from anxiety, there is little that you can do to help yourself. A prisoner may not even understand that what he/she is experiencing is anxiety, fearing it to be some kind of madness. It can develop quite suddenly. For this reason, prisoners may cope with anxiety in different ways. They may feel the tension rising, and being unable to understand, explain or cure it, they may shout at an officer or another prisoner, they may hit out, smash the cell or injure themselves. Some prisoners who set fire to their cells say that lighting the fire made all their tension flood away: tension changed to relaxation. They may do these things for other reasons, of course, but it is important to remember that prisoners do not have the usual means of coping with anxiety. They may behave in bizarre or disruptive ways because they have no other outlet for their tension. In Chapter 9 methods of helping prisoners with anxiety will be described and explained.

Depression

Anxiety and depression may occur at the same time. Just as everyone experiences anxiety at some time, so do most of us feel 'down' from time to time. If you live at home, then there are ways in which you can cope with these feelings. As with anxiety, you can confide in someone and tell them why you feel miserable. You can go out to meet other people, go for a drink, have a game of golf or go fishing. You can go out to the shops and buy yourself something as a treat. Any of these might cheer you up. If you are more seriously depressed, you could take a holiday, or go to a doctor and seek treatment, then take sick leave until you have time to recover. If a prisoner becomes depressed, however, the options for dealing with it are limited. There are fewer opportunities to talk, there is no chance to get away or escape from the situation, and no way of doing something which is fun or really pleasurable. Because the prisoner is limited in what he or she can do about depression, the reaction may be more unusual. It may take the form of withdrawing from other people, being uncommunicative or hostile, and refusing to work. With depression, a prisoner may feel permanently tired, may sleep badly and lack energy, so that they cannot concentrate properly or work efficiently. They will often describe feelings of hopelessness about the future, and may even talk of suicide. In Chapter 9 there is a more detailed description of depression and what can be done to help someone with such a problem.

Suicide

Suicide is the most profound, alarming and confusing form of psychological disturbance. In the general population, people who deliberately injure themselves, by cutting their wrists, or taking an overdose of drugs, for example, have often suffered from depression. This is the same with people who commit suicide, and who see death as their only escape. In prison, this is not necessarily so. Many people who injure themselves and even those who commit suicide do not seem to have been depressed beforehand. This makes it very difficult to predict who is most at risk of suicide.

We know from studies that there are certain times in a prison sentence when a prisoner is at greater risk of committing suicide. Being on remand makes a person vulnerable, and during the first part of a sentence. These are the times when most suicides happen.

It is very difficult to prevent suicides. Nevertheless, every effort should be made to help those who appear to be at risk. If a member of staff thinks that a prisoner is vulnerable, they should tell colleagues and those in charge and steps should be taken to help the prisoner. Some prisons still put prisoners at risk in an isolated cell where all dangerous items have been removed, including sheets, light fittings etc. In other prisons, those at risk are put in the prison hospital where they may be in a ward with others for company. This is the sort of treatment that would occur in an ordinary hospital for someone who was thought to be suicidal. They are very closely observed, and always have someone with them. In this way they have the opportunity to discuss their problems in a safe place.

If a prisoner does commit suicide, it can have a very disturbing effect on those who were either in charge or involved with the prisoner. Many people feel guilty. They think that they ought to have prevented it. They keep thinking of what happened just before the suicide, and wondering if there were any clues which could have told them that the person was suicidal. This is a common reaction to suicide and it also happens with people living in the community. It is perfectly understandable, but it often causes unnecessary suffering. No matter how careful people are, there will always be someone who is really determined and who succeeds in committing suicide. If this happens in prison, those staff who were involved with the prisoner should have the opportunity to discuss these thoughts and feelings with other members of staff. Otherwise they may suffer unnecessary guilt.

Self-injury

The picture is also confusing with those who deliberately harm themselves but do not die. This can happen at any time, and often occurs quite unexpectedly. Some people call it 'parasuicide'. It includes behaviours like cutting the wrists, taking overdoses, jumping off galleries etc.

Deliberate self-injury may happen for several reasons:

1) It could be a suicide attempt that has not succeeded. The prisoner may have felt so bad that he or she really wanted to die.
2) The prisoner may not deliberately plan to kill him or herself but does not care one way or the other.
3) A prisoner may do it in order to exercise some control over his or her circumstances; for example, if the prisoner is about to be moved to another prison or another hall, and does not wish to go. He or she may see it as a means of getting staff to pay attention. Staff naturally become very concerned about self-injury and it therefore has a powerful effect on prison administration.
4) The prisoner may need to talk to a member of staff privately over personal worries and cannot think of another way of being noticed. Such behaviour has often been termed 'manipulative', because the prisoner seems to be trying to manipulate prison authorities to agree with his or her wishes. It is not a very helpful term to use, because it implies that the prisoner is not serious in a desire to get help, but is merely out to cause trouble. Often, however, the prisoner is using the tactic because he or she sees no

other possible solution. Prisoners may be quite desperate in their bid to alter their circumstances. Because they are in prison, they are limited in what they can do to control the situation, so they are more likely to use unusual methods.

There are other forms of self-injury that are not life-threatening, such as friction burning (rubbing the skin so often that it burns or chafes), swallowing items, or scratching the surface of the skin repeatedly. This can happen in response to other kinds of problems; for example, bullying, or family problems outside the prison. Sometimes the prisoner deliberately harms him or herself and does not even consider what will happen afterwards. It is a sudden, impulsive act without a thought for the consequences. The prisoner may not know why he or she did it.

Sometimes the act of injury, for example, cutting or burning the skin, gives the prisoner a feeling of relief of tension. They may have experienced increasing feelings of anxiety and tension, which are relieved as the skin is cut and the prisoner sees the blood coming through. Although this is unusual, when someone has developed the habit of using self-injury to relieve tension, it is difficult for them to break the habit. This type of behaviour tends to be most common among young offenders and among female prisoners.

It is often difficult to know why people have injured or killed themselves. Although it may be as a result of depression, in prison it is more often a response to the stresses of being in prison. If someone reports feeling suicidal, or injures themselves, then it is important to try to find out the reasons. Only then can you decide on the best form of management. It is not easy, but possible methods are described in Chapter 9. It should always be taken seriously. Even prisoners who have no intention of killing themselves, and who merely wish someone to notice them and help them, may injure themselves in a way which results in death. This is particularly true of hanging, which is very quickly fatal.

Lack of communication

As described earlier, prisoners find themselves in a very different environment after admission to a prison. They adapt in a number of ways. One common way is to withdraw and keep themselves to themselves. It is difficult to find someone to trust and it may seem easier to take no risks and avoid confiding in anyone inside prison. This may work well until the prisoner has a personal problem, and then it becomes a strain. Feelings may build up and there is little opportunity to express them or share concerns. If this continues, then anxiety builds up until it reaches a point where the prisoner decides that he or she has to let go of the tension. This may take many of the forms already described for the problem of anxiety: they may become violent, abusive, destructive to property, or they may injure themselves. It may seem obvious that they ought to have spoken to someone about the problem, but for prisoners who are distrustful and find it hard to communicate, it is not the obvious solution.

There may be opportunities for the prisoner to speak to a social worker, or a psychologist or psychiatrist, but these people may not be on hand at the time of a crisis. They may not know the prisoner particularly well. For this reason, it is important that there are opportunities for prisoners to speak privately to officers.

Many officers know their charges well, and may have known them for a long time, through previous time served in prison. If officers have shown themselves to be straightforward and trustworthy, then the prisoner can confide in someone who is going to be there most often, and who knows how to respond to the prisoner. It is one of the hardest aspects of a prison officer's job, but it is also one of the most important. If there is good communication between staff and inmates then both are more secure. The prisoner knows that there is someone around who is prepared to listen, and staff know what is going on in the prison. They are thus more likely to be able to predict the behaviour of their prisoners. Techniques to help individual communication are described in Chapter 8.

This kind of communication does not come automatically in prison. It is something that must be achieved through a deliberate effort to create the right sort of environment. Staff must be encouraged to include this in their role as prison officers, and they must be given the time and opportunity to develop these skills. It is much more subtle and not as easily recognised as the other parts of the job.

One of the problems that must be overcome in talking with prisoners is their feeling of 'paranoia'. The term is used here in the popular, everyday sense, and not in the formal psychiatric sense. The prisoner may suspect that people are trying to take advantage of him or her, and that they will exploit any information that is given. In some cases the prisoner may well be right. In such an unusual environment, it is not surprising to see how this feeling may develop. A prison is a closed institution, where gossip and rumour abound, and there are those who are intent on exploiting any information. In dealing with prisoners, then, there must be a realistic account of how things are. The prisoner may realise, after discussion, that it is fairly safe to talk about some of his worries, but that other issues are just too sensitive to be shared with anyone. There is no reason why prisoners should have to reveal their innermost secrets, but it may help them to reveal some private thoughts and concerns so that staff can help.

Summary

In this chapter, the various effects of imprisonment have been described. They will affect each prisoner in a different way. In some cases the effects will be small, particularly if the imprisonment is for a short period only. With other prisoners, the psychological effects of coming into prison can be quite devastating. They might range from mild anxiety to feelings of utter despair and thoughts of suicide. It is an important part of a prison officer's role to be aware of the prisoner's response and how this might change. Other members of prison staff who come into contact with the inmates can also offer assistance in understanding the effects of imprisonment, but it is likely to be the uniformed officer or an instructor in daily contact who can be of greatest assistance.

Coming into prison to serve a sentence is frequently damaging to prisoners. If they are to have the opportunity of coping with life outside afterwards, then those who work in prisons should try to keep this damage to a minimum. This means reducing the psychological disturbance as much as possible. The result of this will not only benefit the prisoners, but make for a more peaceful prison.

Chapter seven

The impact of AIDS on prison life

It is hard to imagine that there is anybody in this country who will not have heard of AIDS. To that extent the government campaign has done its job. You can hardly switch on your radio or television or open a newspaper without hearing about it. AIDS is well known as the twentieth century plague. There is much good and valid information and discussion on the subject but there is also much scaremongering and many myths. Anxiety and fear is common amongst prisoners and prison officers alike. Much of this fear is founded on confusion. This chapter will attempt to sort out the facts from the fiction and will consider some of the implications for work in prisons.

AIDS is different from many illnesses, not just because there is no cure or vaccine for it, at present, but for a number of other reasons. The first and perhaps the most important of these is that it is difficult to identify. It does not produce certain clearly-defined symptoms, like measles for example. When someone has been infected with the AIDS virus it is not obvious to other people. Indeed, the person affected may not even know. Secondly, someone who thinks that they may have been infected may be reluctant to seek help through fear of the seriousness of the illness or because it may be difficult for them to admit how they caught it. Unlike measles or cancer, AIDS has moral implications: others make judgements about someone with AIDS. If you get AIDS it is assumed that you are either homosexual or an intravenous drug user. Thirdly, someone who is not ill but who has been infected by the AIDS virus will face restrictions in their private life. It is difficult for a young person who feels quite healthy to accept that by having unprotected sex they could put another person in great danger.

So we know that AIDS is not like other illnesses. How then does it evoke so much fear? What are the facts about it?

What is AIDS?

AIDS is a virus which attacks the immune system (the body's natural defence against infection). When someone has AIDS they cannot fight off illnesses as they would normally. There are a few specific illnesses which are relatively rare in the general population but which can develop quite easily in people with AIDS. It is noticing these illnesses in individuals that helps doctors to make a diagnosis of AIDS. This is how AIDS, Acquired Immune Deficiency Syndrome, got its name: the collection of symptoms (syndrome) indicating that the body's defence system has been weakened (immune deficiency). The 'Acquired' part of the name simply indicates that it can be transmitted to you; it is not something caused by your genes.

How AIDS is passed on

Many of the myths about AIDS referred to earlier are about how people can get AIDS. To get AIDS you must first be infected with the AIDS-related virus, the human immunodeficiency virus, HIV for short. HIV is transmitted only in very specific ways. You cannot catch AIDS by shaking hands with an infected person, by doing your laundry in the same washing-machine, by using the same cups and plates, even by hugging or kissing that person. HIV can only be passed on if fluids from the body of an infected person (blood or semen or vaginal fluid) which contain the virus pass directly into the body of a person not infected.

People are advised to use condoms when they have sex because they prevent blood and sexual fluids from penetrating the soft walls of the sex organs and passing into the body. Anal sex is most risky because the walls of the rectum (the back passage) can tear easily and bleed. In this way infected semen can pass straight into the bloodstream or infected blood from one partner can pass through the penis into the body of the other.

Any way in which blood from an infected person can enter the bloodstream of another person carries a high risk of passing on the virus. This is how people who have had blood transfusions or who have shared needles and syringes have been infected. Although some people have got AIDS or have been infected with the virus through transfusions of blood or blood products, the Blood Transfusion Service has acted quickly and now screen and treat blood in order to prevent this from happening again. The virus can also be passed from a mother to her baby, either during pregnancy or at birth and perhaps through breast-feeding.

Clearly, if a person has HIV in their bloodstream, they can pass it on to others in the ways described above. The more often a person has unprotected sex or shares needles and syringes, the more likely they are to contract or pass it on.

Fear of infection

John is nineteen years old and sees himself as a woman's man. He has a job as a hospital porter and enjoys this work. Recently the porters heard that they have an AIDS patient in the hospital and they are very concerned about this. They have taken this to the union and wonder about starting industrial action. They have to take dirty linen to the laundry, to remove bags of clinical waste for disposal, wheel patients on trolleys and so on. They are worried that one of them could catch AIDS. The infection control sister for the hospital has assured them that nurses will make sure that there is no danger and that nursing staff will put things in appropriately coloured bags so that they can transport infected materials with special care. John is not sure that it is really safe. He feels quite angry that the hospital can put them at risk in this way. After work, John likes to go to a disco. He is quite good-looking and always manages to pick up a girl. He doesn't want to settle down just yet and has had a number of short sexual relationships including several 'one-night stands'. He doesn't bother to use a condom as he thinks that would spoil the experience.

John's case is perhaps a bit dramatic but illustrates how people can be concerned about protecting themselves from AIDS in certain situations but don't have the same worries in other parts of their lives. In John's case, he was probably at very little risk at work. There may have been AIDS patients in the hospital but this had been thought about and policies had been drawn up to protect staff, even those who were unlikely to be exposed to the infection. On the other hand, having unprotected sex with a number of partners, especially if you do not know them very well, is much more likely to put you in danger of being infected with the AIDS virus.

Who is at risk?

Practically everything that has been written about AIDS to date defines 'at risk groups', that is, certain groups of people who have a higher incidence of HIV infection and AIDS than others. These groups are: people from certain parts of Africa and Haiti, homosexual men, intravenous drug users, haemophiliacs and others who had blood transfusions at the time when the virus was spreading but before blood products had been treated. The sexual partners of all of these people are also in a high-risk group.

As time passes it makes less sense to identify these high-risk groups. Let us think about why that might be.

1) As mentioned earlier, some people were infected with the virus by blood transfusions. Although this cannot be undone, the number of people who have been exposed to the virus in this way will not increase since action has been taken to ensure that blood supplies do not contain the AIDS-related virus.

2) There are certainly still parts of the world where AIDS is prevalent but as time goes by other countries will be added to the list. Already in places like San Francisco there is a large number of AIDS sufferers and people with HIV infection and we are beginning to trace the spread throughout Great Britain. It is therefore becoming more difficult to say that the virus is confined mainly to specific parts of the world.

3) Similarly, AIDS was seen as the 'gay plague' until around 1984. It is true that the virus has spread fairly widely in the homosexual population but it has crossed over to heterosexuals also. A person cannot get AIDS just by being gay. A homosexual man who has had a faithful relationship with his partner for seven or eight years would not be likely to have HIV infection. In contrast, a promiscuous heterosexual person is at quite a high risk of becoming infected. Homosexual women are at less risk than homosexual men and are probably at less risk than many heterosexual women. It is also true that the rate of infection amongst gay men is no longer rising as before, perhaps because they have been quick to learn about AIDS and to make changes in their behaviour.

4) Finally, drug-takers are at risk of HIV infection through drug use only if they, or their sexual partners, inject drugs with shared needles and syringes. There is some danger in sharing other equipment for injecting. This group of people has been singled out for much attention and has been the target of many

educational campaigns. In addition to this, resources have been put into providing clean needles and syringes for those who cannot, or do not want to, stop injecting. Like the other groups we have described, this group too is becoming less well defined and we are becoming less able to identify who might be carrying HIV.

How can we know who is infected?

For people working in prisons and hospitals, for ambulance drivers and policemen, or anyone in close contact with the public, AIDS has become a major issue. Understandably, these people want to know how to protect themselves and one of the ways they feel they can do so is by finding out who is or who may be infected by the AIDS-related virus. For the last year or two the rule-of-thumb has been to suspect that anyone in a high-risk group may be infected. But how do you know if someone being admitted to hospital is homosexual? Would you always find out if a new prisoner had a girlfriend who injected drugs? Given that the idea of high-risk groups is less useful than it was, is there an alternative way of finding out who is infected? Many people believe that the answer lies in screening, that is, testing a large number of people to detect all those infected by the AIDS virus. Before discussing how people in public service, particularly prison officers, can protect themselves, the problems of how to detect the virus will be discussed.

Detecting the AIDS virus

At present there is no test for AIDS. There is, however, a blood test which can detect the presence of antibodies to HIV, often known as the HIV test. What does this mean, then? The answer is rather complicated; to understand it, we must follow what goes on in the body after infection. When the virus enters a person's bloodstream, the immune system recognises it as a foreign body and reacts to it, producing a chemical substance known as an antibody. With certain infections, antibodies produced can protect us from illness but with HIV infection this is not the case. The antibodies merely indicate that the body has been infected. That person may become ill with AIDS or may remain well but able to pass the infection on to others. Someone who has been infected with the virus and therefore has HIV antibodies in their bloodstream is said to be HIV antibody positive, or just antibody positive. It is possible to be antibody positive for an indefinite amount of time without actually becoming ill with AIDS.

Derek is a heroin user. He is 27 years old now but started using drugs ten years ago. At first he dabbled a little in cannabis and amphetamines but then started smoking heroin and for the last three years has been injecting it. He is married with a three-year-old son. He usually keeps his own needles and syringes but has shared a few times in the past when he has been desperate. Some weeks ago he saw a friend of his who had been in hospital. He looked terrible – very thin and pale, no more than skin and bones; he walked like an old man even though he is the same age as Derek. He stopped to talk and was horrified when this friend said that he had AIDS and had caught it from a shared needle and syringe. Derek got worried and went to his local Community Drugs Team who counselled him and arranged a test. He still hasn't got over the result; he is antibody positive. He can't believe it because he feels fine but he knows he could get ill in the future and can pass it on to others. His wife is too scared to go for the test so when they have sex Derek uses a condom. He feels guilty that he could have infected her and it's difficult to live with the thought that he might go on to get AIDS itself.

Someone like Derek could remain well for months or years before developing full-blown AIDS. The research findings are as yet unclear as to whether AIDS is inevitable and, indeed, how long antibody positive people are likely to remain well. When someone who is antibody positive does become ill with AIDS they are likely to die within a couple of years.

What the HIV test can and cannot tell

We can say that someone who has a positive result on the HIV test is antibody positive. They may not have full-blown AIDS; indeed, they may never get it, but this is not the whole story.

If someone is negative, does this mean that they are in the clear? Again the answer is complex. As you will remember, the test detects the presence of antibodies in the blood. However, the body takes some time to make antibodies in sufficient quantity to show up on the test. For many people this takes place in four to six weeks. The majority of people will show a positive test result after three months but in a few cases this process has been known to take longer. We can't then be sure that someone who has a negative test result has not been infected with

HIV if they were in a risky situation (had unprotected sex, shared needles, etc.) in the previous three months at least.

Clearly, even in prisons we cannot guarantee that this is the case for many of the inmates, at least for those serving short sentences and for all those who have just been brought into custody.

How do we tell when someone has AIDS?

When someone is in the early stages of full-blown AIDS, it is often difficult even for a doctor to diagnose. As mentioned earlier in this chapter, AIDS is a gradual breakdown of the immune system and may show itself in different ways. At the start it is usually seen as swollen glands, tiredness and lethargy: common symptoms of the start of many illnesses. The HIV blood test may be helpful to doctors for diagnosis if it is not known whether or not a patient is antibody positive.

If someone has full-blown AIDS, they are no more infectious than a person who is antibody positive (unless of course they have diarrhoea or there is some other chance of infection from loss of body fluids). When a person who is antibody positive begins to be ill, it is important that they receive medical treatment as soon as possible as minor infections can be cured. For every person who has AIDS, however, there are several others who are antibody positive but otherwise healthy. They too could pass on the infection to other people.

How can we protect ourselves?

We started off by saying that some people think that we can protect ourselves by screening. By this they mean that a large number of people should be tested to find out who is antibody positive. Let us look at the reasons why this idea is not as good as it first seems:

1) Who do you test? We have already looked at the high-risk groups and have considered how they are becoming less easy to define.
2) Even if we decide to start with the high-risk groups, how do we trace them? Are gay men and intravenous drug users going to come forward for testing? Do we wait until they come into the hospital or prison systems, and then can we be sure of identifying all of those in the high-risk groups?
3) If we abandon the idea of high-risk groups, do we then take on the enormous expense of testing everyone?

4) If we do test people in order to protect ourselves, what do we do with those people who are found to be antibody positive?

5) How far can screening take us? As we have already learnt, a negative test result could mean that a person is infected but has not yet made sufficient antibodies to be detected by the test. Not only do we need to test them again after about three months but we also have to make sure that they avoid unprotected sex and/or 'risky' intravenous drug use during that three-month period.

6) Identifying antibody positive people might make us less careful about others. Someone may have been infected with the virus and we may not know the results of the test or the result may be negative at the time of testing. If this is the case, we could put ourselves at more risk by thinking that we need only take precautions with those people whom we know are antibody positive.

7) All this suggests that we would require to take precautions against infection from a large number of people even if we did have screening. In this case, would we gain very much from testing?

If testing is not the answer, then what can we do to make sure that we can protect ourselves from being infected with the AIDS virus?

Taking precautions

Earlier we described how the AIDS virus is passed on. As it is transmitted from one person to another in very specific ways it is not easy to catch in normal daily contact with others.

It is sensible for anyone who works closely with people to observe standard rules of hygiene, for example, washing your hands if you have been in contact with body fluids from another person. Covering even small cuts, especially on your hands, with a plaster is also important to make sure that the AIDS virus has no access to your bloodstream. If you know you will be in a situation where there is likely to be blood or other body fluids around, plastic or rubber gloves should be used.

Perhaps the most threatening thing for a prison officer is the unexpected fight or attack. In such a situation, an officer may be cut or scratched and the prisoner or prisoners may also be bleeding. Here the officer could be open to possible infection. In difficult circumstances such as these there can be no guarantees. The best way of protecting oneself is, of course, to try to avoid such conflict. Chapters 5 and 10 discuss how to avoid or reduce aggression. Usual methods of restraint should minimise the risks. In the unfortunate circumstance of an officer being injured and a prisoner's blood coming on or near the wound, what should be done? There are two simple procedures to follow: (1) encourage the wound to bleed by squeezing, and (2) wash the wound thoroughly.

If blood has been spilt in a struggle, it should be cleaned up as soon as possible. Anyone who is wiping surfaces on which blood has been spilt should wear plastic or rubber gloves. If paper towels are available, they may be used to mop up initially as they can be easily incinerated. After the blood has been removed and the surface rinsed, it should be disinfected with household bleach. It is normally recommended that a solution of one measure of bleach in nine measures of water is used. As bleaches may vary in concentration according to brand, a slightly stronger solution may be better, providing that the surfaces will not be damaged by it.

It cannot be repeated too often that we cannot always know who is infected by the AIDS virus. The precautions which must be taken to protect ourselves from infection are simple. By using them at all times we will not be taking any chances with our health.

Controlling AIDS

Thus far we have discovered how we can protect ourselves from catching AIDS in the work-place. Testing a large number of people is, we have seen, neither a practical nor sufficient precaution. The fairly simple practices described above should be sufficient to protect us. Returning to John, the hospital porter we encountered earlier in the chapter, he was safe at work but could be at risk of HIV infection in his private life. This illustrated how people can very often ignore risks when they are not pointed out to them. Being aware of AIDS at work does not mean that we can stop it from spreading. Individuals are most likely to be infected by the virus at times when they are away from work.

Diseases such as smallpox and polio which were a great threat to people's lives one or two generations ago have been controlled very effectively with vaccines. For AIDS, however, there is no vaccine. Doctors and scientists are working on such a solution but it may be several years before one is developed. It may be even longer before it is available to the general population.

The only hope that we have of controlling AIDS at present is if people change their behaviour. When we are talking of sexual behaviour, a change is difficult to enforce. If we cannot make people change what they do, we can at least encourage them to do so. We can try to do this first by educating people to understand what AIDS is and how it is transmitted.

Then, if possible, they should be encouraged to think about how this applies to them personally. The government campaigns and leaflets published by organisations such as the Terrence Higgins Trust provide the necessary information. It is much more difficult, however, to make this message more personal and is best done through discussions with individuals or in small groups.

The prisoner and AIDS

AIDS has been a particular problem in the last year or two in British prisons. One of the major reasons for this is that prisons house a much larger proportion of people in high-risk groups than is found in the general population, primarily drug users imprisoned for drug-related offences. Prisons therefore are ideal situations for educating people who may well come into contact with the virus. Not only can information be made available on a large scale but also facilities exist, through education units, for example, to talk to inmates alone or in small groups about how AIDS does, or could, affect them personally.

Many prisoners will consider themselves as perhaps being or having been at risk from infection by the AIDS virus and may ask for the HIV test. Alternatively, other people may wish them to be tested for a number of reasons. If someone is to have the HIV test, it is important that they discuss the test with a qualified counsellor beforehand. The counsellor will ensure that they understand what the test can and cannot tell them and will give advice on how to protect themselves and/or others in the future. The counsellor will also help a person to assess for themselves the degree of risk they have been exposed to and will encourage them to anticipate how they might react if the result of the test was positive. Finally, the counsellor will arrange for the HIV test to be carried out only with the consent of that person. Even if someone is likely to have been infected with the AIDS-related virus, it is not always a good idea to carry out the HIV test. A surprising number of people do not want to know and are prepared to change their life-styles anyway, so for them the test may not be relevant. For others who perhaps have not coped well with bad news in the past, it is probably better that they do not know. If telling someone that he is antibody positive might cause him to be so upset that he begins to behave irrationally, it may be less dangerous simply not to test him but to encourage him as much as possible to alter his risky behaviour.

Before anyone has the HIV antibody test, they should give their informed consent. That is, they should understand what the test is about and agree to it. There has been much discussion about this, particularly in organisations such as the British Medical Association. It seems that, legally, no blood can be taken from someone without telling them why. Although this is not formally done for many routine blood tests, there are a number of pressure groups such as gay rights organisations who have helped people bring charges of assault on doctors who have taken blood for testing without consent.

Individuals must also give their consent for a doctor to tell anyone else of their HIV test result or indeed of the fact that they have had a test. In this situation doctors are not only bound by the rules of confidentiality but also by the 1974 V.D. Act, which also applies to AIDS as it can be sexually transmitted. Services, then, may be provided in prisons for taking care of antibody positive people, for testing individuals who may have been infected and for educating prisoners, giving them information, helping them to think of the implications for themselves and how they might change their behaviour.

Summary

AIDS (Acquired Immune Deficiency Syndrome) is a collection of different symptoms which, typically, are noted when the body's natural defence against illness breaks down.

The cause of AIDS is infection with the human immunodeficiency virus (HIV). A person can be infected with this virus either through sex or when infected body fluids from another person pass directly into his or her bloodstream through breaks in the skin or through the sex organs.

When someone is infected with the AIDS-related virus, their body makes antibodies which can be detected by a blood test, the HIV antibody test. If a person has a positive result from the HIV test, they are said to be antibody positive. An antibody positive person may not have AIDS but may develop the illness in the future and can pass the virus on.

Testing a large number of people for HIV antibodies is not a solution to controlling the spread of AIDS. At present, the best methods available for limiting AIDS are education, discussion to encourage individuals to think personally about the disease and helping people to change their behaviour.

Chapter eight

Communication skills

Human actions determine human reactions. If you are aggressive to a prisoner he will be aggressive back, if you are relaxed he will relax too. Good prison officers are good communicators: they can calm prisoners when they are 'high', they can persuade them when they are difficult, they can support them when they are bereaved. Some officers think that prisoners should be shouted at, all orders being liberally sprinkled with four-letter words. Any other approach is seen as being soft. Good communication is not soft. Good communication is effective. It helps to diffuse the tension in the prison, it reduces the chances of riots, hostage-takings and other demonstrations, prisoners will do what they are told – with fewer complaints – and day-to-day problems are sorted out before they are blown out of proportion. Good communication improves your job performance. It will also improve your job satisfaction. Prison life will be easier for everyone.

Improving communication skills

We all know people who seem to be born communicators. They can talk to anyone, they are interested in what other people have to say, they can persuade people to do things with no apparent effort, they are relaxed with people. Don't despair. Communication skills are like any other skills – driving a car, hitting a golf ball or laying bricks – they can be learned. If you are going to learn a skill, first, you have to find out what to do, second, you have to practise it and third, you have to see what result you get. In this chapter we will tell you some of the things you can do to improve your communication skills. It will be up to you to practise them and to monitor how effective you are.

What communication skills are important in prisons?

The good communicator will have a variety of skills. Some are easy to learn, some are more difficult. The best way to learn any skill is to start with the basic parts first and then add on the more complicated parts. When you are learning to drive a car, you start by concentrating on steering before moving on to learning how to change gear efficiently. With communication skills we will start by describing observation skills, then we will consider how you can be a good listener before going on to talk about giving orders and how to be assertive without being aggressive. We will start with the easiest skill, observation.

Observation

Observation is the foundation on which all communication skills are based. Observing other people's behaviour tells you when to be more relaxed or when to be firm, it tells you when someone is sad or when someone is feeling aggressive. It helps you to understand behaviour. It helps you to keep out of trouble.

George was a new recruit. He had been in the army so his boots were polished, his buttons were shining and he reckoned he could look after himself. George thought that one prisoner is much the same as any other; he just locked them up at night and let them out in the morning. He did not pay them much attention. One morning, when he was organising 'slopping out', a prisoner came up to him and asked quietly for a letter. George told him to 'bugger off' and get on with slopping out. Without warning, the prisoner attacked George, thrashing him.

It appeared to George that he had been attacked without warning; however, his Principal Officer standing nearby was not surprised. Although the prisoner had asked for a letter in a quiet and polite way, he had asked through clenched teeth. As he came up to George his muscles were straining out of his jacket, his eyes were bright and wide, he looked as if he couldn't stand still. The P.O. had watched the prisoner before and knew that he was usually calm, relaxed and cheerful, whereas now he was wound up like a coiled spring. George was surprised by the attack, the observant P.O. was not.

Being observant is important. Prisoners may be reluctant to discuss their problems with officers. If you are observant you can spot a prisoner's difficulties and approach him or be prepared to meet any difficulties should they emerge. How do you become more observant?

There are two important parts to observation. First, you collect the information which you require and secondly, you draw conclusions from this information. If you see a prisoner staring out another prisoner you might come to the conclusion that they were angry with each other. If a prisoner who normally talks to you starts avoiding you, he may be under pressure from other inmates or he may be annoyed with something you've done.

When you are collecting information you should try to answer several questions. First, think about the prisoner's behaviour: what is he doing at the moment? Is he keeping busy, is he walking up and down, is he arguing with his best friend, is he keeping out of the way of the heavy team? Second, think about the prisoner's appearance: is he tense, is he angry, is he withdrawn, does he look unkempt? Third, think about his context: where is he hanging about, who is he with?

Try to answer these questions in as concrete a manner as possible. Avoid 'fuzzies', think and talk in terms of 'performances'. A 'fuzzy' is a vague or imprecise description such as 'Joe's got a poor attitude' or 'Jimmy lost the place'. If you use these 'fuzzy' descriptions then the person you are talking to doesn't really know what Joe and Jimmy are doing wrong. They do not know what to look out for, they do not know what to discuss with Joe or Jimmy. If you are talking to the prisoner in a fuzzy way, 'You'd better pull up your socks, and get a grip', then you are not telling the prisoner what to do to change. He might take you literally.

Think and talk in terms of 'performances'. Performances are precise descriptions of what people have done and what they are doing. 'Joe's got a poor attitude' would be better described as 'Joe always argues back when he is told to get up or is told to go to work'. A performance describes what he does and when he does it in concrete terms. 'Jimmy lost the place' might be more accurately described as 'Jimmy started shouting and bawling and tried to hit the Principal Officer'. Anyone listening to this description would have a clearer idea of what actually happened. If you think and talk in terms of performances rather than fuzzies then you communicate more accurately and you think more clearly.

The second part of observation – the most important part – is making inferences. When you make inferences you use the information which you have collected to work out how the prisoner is feeling, what his relationships are like with other people and how he is likely to behave in the future. If you can work out how someone is feeling – using what you have observed – then you can predict how they might behave. The

Principal Officer in the example above worked out that the prisoner was tense. He had observed the strained muscles, the clenched teeth, the eyes which were wide and bright. He was not surprised when the prisoner attacked George. Good observation keeps you out of trouble.

You should observe relationships: relationships between prisoners and relationships between prisoners and officers. Relationships give clues about future action. Prisoners who avoid officers or who tend to be hostile or argumentative may cause problems in the future. Prisoners who develop easy and relaxed relationships with officers may give valuable information.

Relationships among prisoners are also important. Every prison has its competing groups of prisoners. You should try to observe which prisoners belong to which groups. If old friends are not hanging around together this may mean trouble. If members of different groups start bumping or staring each other down this might also mean trouble.

Observation is the basic skill you need before you start being a good communicator. If you can observe well, then you know how to pitch your communication, you know whether to be soft or hard, whether you should deal with a problem immediately or whether you should allow time to cool off. Try practising observation. With practice it will become an automatic skill.

Listening skills

When people think about communication they usually think about talking. Communication is not just about talking; it is also about listening. People who are good listeners can calm people down, can help people through crises such as a bereavement or a 'knock back'; they can build the rapport that helps the smooth running of a jail and they can keep in touch with what the prisoner is thinking. Good prison officers are good listeners.

How do you become a good listener? We will describe five skills which you can learn, namely, body language, verbal cues, reflection, self-disclosure and being accepting.

Body language

When we communicate with people we don't just use words, we also use our bodies. Body language is the language of our eyes, our gestures, our posture and our facial expressions. Body language can change the meaning of our words. Someone might say 'You're doing well Jimmy', but his body language – the way he smiles, the way he uses his hands and his eyes – will tell you if he really means it, or whether he is being sarcastic. Good communicators need to be as good at body language as they are at using spoken language.

When you are listening, what body language should you use? When you are listening your body language is used to show the other person that you are paying attention and are interested in what they are saying. To achieve this you should lean towards the other person, stand reasonably still and avoid fidgeting. You should look at the person, rather than watching what else is going on around you. You are interested in what they are telling you, not what other people are doing. The way you look at other people needs some care; if you look for too long it becomes a stare – it becomes aggressive. Good listeners will nod their heads to signal that they are listening and will smile to encourage the other person to keep going.

Verbal cues

It is often said that 'it's not what you say but the way that you say it' which is important. The tone of your voice can change the 'message' you give when you say something. Just to prove this to yourself go somewhere quiet and try saying 'I've lost my socks' in an angry way, a sad way and a relaxed way. See how your voice tone changes the message. When you are listening your tone should be warm and calm. There should be no trace of boredom, hostility or impatience.

Other verbal cues are important. If you watch a chat show on television you will notice that the interviewer will be following what his guest is saying and will signal this by brief verbal cues such as 'I see', 'uh huh', and 'that's interesting'. These cues keep the other person talking. The interviewer's job is to ask questions, but if you watch you will see that he does not ask any old questions; he will concentrate on 'open questions'. Open questions are questions which can't be answered 'yes' or 'no'; open questions require longer answers – they keep the other person talking. So you might ask a prisoner after a visit 'How was your family?' (open question) rather than 'Was your family all right?' (closed question). With the first question you should get more information, with the second the prisoner may just answer 'yes' or 'no'. Questions are important but they need to be used with care. Too many questions – or the wrong questions – can make a prisoner clam up.

Before leaving verbal cues, we should consider silence. Silence isn't really a verbal cue but it is very important. It is one of the most powerful ways of getting people to talk. Inexperienced listeners often find silences hard to tolerate. They have to say something because they find that silence makes them tense. If you can remain silent it will help and encourage the other person to say some more.

Reflection

We use the word reflection to describe what the good listener does to show the other person that he is getting the message. Reflection shows that the listener understands what the prisoner is saying or what he is feeling. The prisoner should feel that he is standing in front of a large mirror with his ideas and feelings being bounced back at him. That is reflection.

How do you reflect? The easiest way is to repeat back what the person said, perhaps changing some of their words. If a prisoner said, 'The f---ing governor won't see me', you might reflect the content by saying, 'So the governor is not going to see you', and you might reflect what he is feeling by saying, 'So you're angry at the governor'. This improves your listening skill in four ways: you show the prisoner that you're paying attention, you encourage him to talk without having to ask a question, you can summarise and clarify what is bothering him, and finally, you show that you understand what he is feeling. At first, reflection is quite a difficult skill to use because it feels a bit artificial. With practice it becomes natural and very effective.

Self-disclosure

Self-disclosure means saying something about yourself, your experiences or your interests. It is a way of developing trust, it helps to break down barriers and encourages the prisoner to be more open and honest. If one partner in a conversation always withholds personal information, the other partner is less likely to reveal personal details. We are not suggesting that you reveal very personal information but just routine information about your interests outside and your experiences which might be similar to that of the prisoner. An example might be:

Prisoner: 'I flared up because I've been worrying about my son going into hospital. He went in for an operation yesterday and I still don't know if he's all right.'

Officer: 'I can see why you're upset, it's very worrying. None of my kids has ever been in hospital, but last year when my wife went in for a check-up, I was really on edge. I kept

shouting at the kids. It's not knowing what's happening
that really gets to you.'

Prisoner: 'Yes, that's it, feeling uncertain and thinking that they are
not really telling you everything. I always get uptight if I
think that people are keeping things from me. That's when
I find myself getting out-of-hand and causing trouble.'

When the officer disclosed something about himself – the fact that he
got upset when his wife was in hospital – it encouraged the prisoner to
say more. If the officer had just said 'I know what it's like but there's no
point in worrying', the prisoner might have felt put down and not have
said anymore. By disclosing something which is slightly personal the
prison officer encouraged the prisoner to disclose more information
about himself – the fact that he gets angry when people withhold
information from him. The more you know about prisoners the more
effective you can be in your job. Self-disclosure does not have to be
exactly equal on both sides. As long as there is some exchange of
personal experience, the effect should be beneficial.

Being accepting

Being accepting is the most difficult listening skill. By being accepting
we mean that you recognise that someone has the right to feel whatever
they feel, although they do not necessarily have the right to do whatever
they like. If a prisoner gets a 'knock back' on his request for parole, we
can accept that he has a right to feel angry and disappointed but we
cannot accept that he should 'smash up'. Accepting other people means
understanding their feelings, without being critical. You can still
disagree with what they do, and you can tell them so. Good listeners tune
into and accept other people's feelings. How can you show that you are
accepting?

Officer: 'I can see why you're upset with not getting a date,
especially as you've kept your nose clean for the last
couple of years. Anyone would be upset by that. But you
can't go around threatening to put people in the freezer just
because you got a "knock back".'

Prisoner: 'It's diabolical. Everyone else gets out first go. I just
screwed a few houses and they keep me locked up. They
don't know what they are doing.'

Officer: 'Well, I can understand why you're angry, your record's
not that bad. I'll try to find out what went against you and

how you can improve your chances next time, but don't go around threatening people, it won't do you or anyone any good.'

In this example the officer shows that he understands and accepts the prisoner's right to be angry, although he makes it very clear that he cannot accept his threatening behaviour. Accepting people's feelings has a calming effect.

Improving your listening skills will go a long way to improving your man-management skills. You will gain confidence in your ability to calm prisoners down or cope with them when you have to give them bad news. Like any skill, listening needs practice. Start by trying each of the skills one at a time. Experiment, see how your behaviour affects the prisoner's behaviour; when you get more confident start putting the skills together. Like riding a bike, once you learn to be a good listener you will never forget.

Assertion

The prison officer's primary role is to control prisoners. Some prison officers exert control by being aggressive; the good prison officer exerts control by being assertive. Let's return to the basic equation of human behaviour, 'human actions determine human reactions'. If you are aggressive, the prisoner is likely to become aggressive in response. Being assertive means putting your point across without being aggressive, without shouting or bawling at other people. Assertive behaviour means standing up for your rights or, in prisons, telling people what to do without feeling anxious or angry.

It is important to be assertive because you can get your views across without conflict, it stops prisoners from trying to manipulate you and it gives your colleagues confidence in your ability to handle difficult situations. Assertive behaviour has obvious advantages, yet many people don't know how to be assertive. Some reasons for this would include,

1) they do not know what words or phrases to use at the time – although half an hour later they know exactly what they should have said,
2) they are so anxious that they become completely tongue-tied,
3) they are so angry that they can't put their point across reasonably,

4) they believe that the way to get people to do things is to shout at them.

With training and practice it is possible to overcome all these difficulties so that you too can be assertive. How can you become more assertive? We will look at three skills which you should focus on, namely, body language, verbal cues and the 'broken record'.

Body language

We saw earlier that when people communicate they use their bodies – their eyes, their hands, their posture – as well as their words. People who are good at being assertive use their bodies in particular ways. The best posture to adopt is one in which you are standing up straight, your head is up and your shoulders are back. You should stand square on to the person you are talking to – standing still and not fidgeting. It is important to look directly at the person.

Verbal cues

As with most communication, what is important is not what you say but how you say it. When you are being assertive the volume of your voice should be normal; you shouldn't shout as this comes across as anger. The tone of your voice should be steady and firm – show that you mean business – and you should stress important words, e.g. 'You WILL go behind your door NOW'.

The broken record technique

We have described what body language and which verbal cues you should use when you are being assertive. We have described how you say things. Let's consider some of the things you might say.

When you are being assertive you must be persistent. There is no need to become angry or start shouting; just keep saying what you want over and over again until the other person agrees with you or offers a compromise. This is where the broken record technique comes in. When a record is broken the same phrase of music will be repeated again and again. When you are being assertive you should repeat the same phrase again and again. Let us consider an example.

Suppose, just before you lock up a prisoner, he demands some paper. It is clearly an inappropriate request. He has had all the recreation period to ask and you are now very busy trying to get everyone behind their doors. One way of dealing with such a request is to bawl him out, get him into his cell and bang the door behind him. He will get the message that you are annoyed, but he may harbour his anger and take it out on the officer who opens him up in the morning. Another way is to use the 'broken record':

Prisoner: Can I have some paper to write a letter?

Officer: I'm sorry you'll have to get into your cell now, you can get some in the morning.

Prisoner: But I need to write a letter.

Officer: You should have asked me earlier. You can get some in the morning.

Prisoner: I had an argument with my wife on the visit this afternoon. I want to write and put things right.

Officer: That's a good idea, but you've had all evening to ask me. You can get some in the morning. The letter will get to her just as quickly.

Prisoner: OK. I suppose you're right. Will you see that I get the paper in the morning?

Officer: Yes, I'll leave a note for the early shift.

The prisoner's request was legitimate but his timing was wrong. You were busy ensuring that everyone was locked up. Security was your primary concern. By sticking to your guns and repeating, 'you can get some in the morning', you got the prisoner to accept your decision without the encounter developing into an argument or something worse. Using the same phrase over and over again can get quite monotonous. You can be just as effective if you vary the words but keep the message the same.

It may be tempting to get prisoners to do things by being aggressive. Try being assertive instead. That way, you get things done and you don't store up problems for the future.

Giving orders

Many of your everyday communications will be orders. For junior staff this means giving orders to prisoners. The purpose of orders is to get the prisoner to do what is necessary. Orders should not be used to make you feel big or the prisoner feel small. Experience shows that calm and polite requests are the most effective way of getting prisoners to do what is required with the least resistance. If you don't give orders properly you are just making more work for yourself and your colleagues. There are officers who feel that if they are polite to prisoners then they will look weak. The opposite is true. If you are polite and the prisoner doesn't respond, he is clearly in the wrong. You have given him the opportunity to do things the easy way, so that it becomes his problem if you have to go the hard way.

When you give an order, make sure that what you say is clear. Don't speak too quickly. Use everyday language instead of jargon or pompous words. If it is a complicated order, get the prisoner to repeat the order back to you. Take time to make sure that they understand what you mean. That saves time in the long term.

Handling requests

Junior officers are the first point of contact that prisoners have with the authorities. Requests will come to you. The way in which requests are handled has a strong effect on the level of tension and violence in prisons. If requests are dealt with fairly then this will help you to establish a reasonable working relationship with prisoners.

There are three important points to remember when dealing with requests. First, don't refuse a request just for the sake of it. If the regime allows something, then the prisoner should be allowed it. Second, if you have to say no, give a reason. If you explain to people then they are less likely to be upset by the refusal. Third, if you grant a request which would not normally be granted, make sure you make it clear why it is being granted on this occasion. Again, give your reason. Talking to prisoners about your decisions is not a sign of weakness. It helps to build rapport and even if you have to refuse requests you will be seen to be fair.

Writing reports

All the above communication skills have dealt with what we say and how we say it. More and more prison officers are having to communicate in writing. Like any other skill writing reports can be difficult to begin with, but with some thought and practice it can become second nature. Usually the reports written by prison officers describe a prisoner's behaviour. Describing the behaviour of other people can be difficult. Accuracy is hard to achieve because the words we use are not precise, our feelings about the prisoner can affect our judgements, the prisoner's behaviour may vary a lot. There are some guidelines which may help your report writing:

1) When describing behaviour avoid 'fuzzies', for example, 'Joe's got a poor attitude', and concentrate on 'performances', for example, 'Joe always argues when he is told to go to work'.
2) For many reports you have to describe the person's behaviour over the previous year. Everyone tends to focus on recent changes – changes in the last month or two – and forget the long-term changes. Do not let recent changes in behaviour – either good or bad – affect your overall judgement.
3) Try to be objective. Focus on facts, not supposition or rumour. Ask yourself, 'have I got information to corroborate or support this view?' If you describe your evidence the reader will be more convinced.
4) Try to put aside your feelings about the individual, your likes and your dislikes. This can be difficult but it is essential if you are going to produce a report of any value.
5) Highlight positive achievements as well as negative.

The above guidelines should help you with the content of your report. What about the style? Reports will be clearer if you use the following guidelines:

1) Keep sentences short, but vary their length.
2) Use common, familiar words – avoid jargon and 'psychobabble'.
3) Use active verbs such as 'Jimmy hit Fred', rather than 'Fred was hit by Jimmy'.
4) Be concrete and specific.
5) Eliminate words you can do without.

Summary

Good communications make prisons work. This is not a new idea dreamt up by psychologists, rather it is the evidence of experience. As far back as 1844, the Inspectors of Prisons for Scotland pointed out 'in some prisons an unusual degree of good conduct is induced, and the number of punishments kept low, by the personal influence of the officers, and by their care in reasoning with prisoners before resorting to punishment'. Good prison officers are good communicators. If you use the hard approach you will get the hard response. Try listening and reasoning. Be assertive rather than aggressive.

Chapter nine

Coping with disturbed prisoners

In Chapter 6, we looked at the psychological effects of being in a prison. In this chapter, we will look at the ways in which prison staff can assist prisoners who are psychologically disturbed. We are not going to describe the various psychiatric illnesses that can affect prisoners, since these are best dealt with by medical and nursing staff. Instead, we are going to describe the more common kinds of psychological disorder and how they might be managed. If you are ever in doubt, you must always refer a prisoner to the medical or psychology staff. Despite this there is still much that an officer can do in gathering helpful information about the prisoner's difficulties and in managing a disturbed or distressed prisoner. It is the staff who are in daily contact with the prisoner and who can have most influence on his or her well-being.

Describing psychological disturbance

In Chapter 8, we outlined how behaviour should be described. We have emphasised how important it is to be precise in your descriptions. Just to remind you, here is an example of what this might mean for someone who is psychologically disturbed. Instead of saying, 'Margaret is refusing to come out from behind her door', you could give more accurate and detailed information; for example, 'Margaret is in her cell and refuses to come out. She is pacing around the room, holding her arms and occasionally digging her fingernails into them. She is tearful and will not answer any questions'.

By giving this more detailed information, we already have a clue that Margaret is tense and agitated. We also know that she is unwilling or unable to talk about what is upsetting her. Just by adding a little more factual description, we have a much better idea of the problem. This would help anyone who had to go to interview her. It would also help the decision of how best to manage her, since her behaviour is indicating that she is either angry, upset or anxious about something. It does not sound as if she is merely refusing to co-operate.

In describing anyone who is psychologically disturbed, it is important to list the facts about them and to describe their behaviour. What is the prisoner actually doing and what does he or she look like? Try to avoid woolly descriptions and generalisations. Be accurate in your description. These general rules apply to all kinds of report writing, but are particularly relevant when you are being asked about someone who may be disturbed. Your information is very important – you have most contact with the prisoner – so present it in the best way.

Changes in behaviour can be important signs. If you know a prisoner well, you will know their habits and the way they normally behave. If the prisoner changes, then you may begin to wonder why this is happening. It may be that he or she is in with a different crowd or that there has been news from outside, but whatever it is, it has changed the prisoner's behaviour and this is worth noting. If a man appears to be very anxious, for example, he is agitated when talking to other people, moving from one foot to the other, clenching his fists and stumbling over his words, then it will be essential to know whether this is usual for him. If he has always behaved like this, then it is less likely that anything has happened recently to upset him. It may be just part of his character. But if he used to be quite relaxed, standing still and chatting without showing any of the signs of anxiety listed above, then you know that he is under stress of some kind.

How do we identify psychological disturbance; what can we do to help the disturbed prisoner? In the next section we will look at the most common forms of psychological disturbance that you will come across in prison.

Anxiety

Anxiety may just be part of your personality, or it may come in response to some kind of stress. Stress may come from any direction: bullying, worry over a future decision about parole, movement to another institution or involvement in illegal activities. It might be concern over what is happening to someone outside, or the prisoner's own health. Some common signs of anxiety resulting from such stress are listed below. Be careful, some of the signs may have other causes: trembling and sweating may happen with a flu virus, or even a more serious illness, but if they occur without other signs of disease, then they may well be caused by anxiety.

Common symptoms of anxiety

headaches	migraine
dizziness	blurred vision
blushing	trembling
twitching	muscle spasms
difficulty in breathing	difficulty in swallowing
aching muscles in neck, back or legs	heart palpitations
heart skipping a beat	thumping chest pains
stomach churning	feeling sick (nausea)
indigestion	butterflies in stomach
tiredness	weak knees
'jelly' legs	sweating
feeling the need to pass water frequently	

You can see from the list that these symptoms are very varied and could be caused by physical illnesses. This is why it is wise to refer a prisoner to medical services to ensure that the cause of their symptoms is known. There might be very serious or tragic consequences if someone who had heart disease, for example, was told that they were merely anxious. We must stress again that people who complain of these symptoms should be seen by a member of the medical staff to ensure that they are properly treated. If it is concluded that they have anxiety then staff can be reassured that there is no underlying physical illness.

If someone is found to be anxious like this, what can you do to help? There are various ways of helping someone and the method you choose will depend on your circumstances. Suppose it is a sudden crisis: an example might be where a prisoner is suddenly very anxious about a visit which will happen on the same day. If there is time, then you can obviously talk about it and find out why the prisoner is worried. But you may not have time. If this is the case, then you can offer the following advice:

1) Breathe slowly and evenly.
2) Sit down if possible and gradually let go of physical tension in:
   a) shoulders (pull them down and back and then let go),
   b) chest (take a deep breath and let it out slowly),

   c) stomach (clench the stomach muscles to make them hard and
      then let go),

   d) legs (stretch them out and then let them flop),

   e) arms (bend your arms at the elbow, pulling your hands up to
      your shoulders and then let go again),

   f) hands (stretch out the five fingers and then let them relax).

3) Keep breathing slowly and evenly. Reassure the prisoner that they
will be all right. Talk to the prisoner: if it does not help to talk
about their fear, then talk about something completely different in
order to distract the prisoner from the worry: talk about the news,
weather, sport, or TV programmes. Ask some questions to try to
get the prisoner involved in your conversation. Stay with the
prisoner until the anxiety subsides.

If you are able to stay longer with the prisoner, or you have the opportunity for a private talk, then use tactics that are known to help people to
talk about problems. These are listening skills. We described these in
Chapter 8 but let us look at how they can be used with someone who is
anxious.

1) Look at the prisoner when he or she is trying to talk to you.

2) Say things to show that you are interested and sympathetic, for
example: 'That must be very difficult for you', 'I think that I can
see why you might be worried', 'You've been under quite a strain
recently'.

3) Reassure the prisoner if you can, for example: 'I think there are
ways of handling it', 'We can probably arrange some help for
that', 'I'll try to help you all I can'.

4) Try to stay calm yourself. If you act as if you are coping with the
situation, the prisoner may well copy you.

If you have tried to help the prisoner to relax, and to talk about the
problem and have not been able to get very far, then you may want to try
something else.

    Sometimes a prisoner may want to talk to someone who is not part of
the hall or block. They may feel that they want to talk to someone who
is different. You might suggest talking to a chaplain, doctor, social
worker, psychologist or psychiatrist. If, at any stage, you are worried
about the prisoner, you should seek a second opinion from someone
else.

Depression

We have talked about stress above and how it may affect people. In many people it will show itself as anxiety: it may also show itself as depression. We talked briefly about depression in Chapter 6. Now we will describe it in more detail. The word depression is not a very good description because it can mean so many different things. There may be times when you feel 'down', you may not feel very cheerful and you may not want to do very much. Some people call this depression. Feeling depressed can range from these mild experiences to being so severe that you stop eating, moving or caring about anything at all. People who are severely depressed may not care whether they go on living or not, or they may decide that death is the only solution. They may try to kill themselves.

In psychiatry, the term 'depression' is usually kept for someone who shows very specific symptoms, and not for someone who is just temporarily 'fed up'. A careful examination must be made to decide how severe the depression is and how the prisoner should be treated. One of the problems when prisoners get depressed is that they cannot summon the energy to go for help. They may believe that no one cares enough to give them help. Prison officers need to be alert to the tell-tale signs of depression so that they can send the prisoner for a thorough medical or psychological examination.

None of the signs below is a sure way of spotting depression, but they should alert a prison officer to find out more, or to seek a second opinion. Some of them are very mild signs but they get more serious as the list goes on:

> feeling miserable
> feeling listless or lacking in energy
> lack of interest in usual activities
> being irritable
> sleeping poorly
> losing interest in food
> losing weight
> feeling guilty over things that are not particularly important
> feeling useless
> feeling hopeless about things
> thinking that things will never get any better
> saying that there is no point in carrying on
> talking about wanting to die

It must be emphasised at this point that if prisoners talk of harming themselves or even killing themselves, this must always be taken seriously. No prison officer can risk misunderstanding a prisoner who may try to kill him or herself.

If you suspect that someone is depressed, seek help. If they are already being treated for depression, or if it is not considered serious enough to warrant medical treatment, then there are ways in which an officer can help, either on a day-to-day basis, or in a longer, private talk.

1) Listen carefully. Try to show that you are interested in the prisoner's difficulties and that you are sympathetic.
2) Try to give hope to the prisoner. Suggest ways in which things might be improved. Do not promise anything that you cannot be sure of, but try to think of ways in which the situation could be helped.
3) If there are practical problems that can be solved, e.g., a change of work, or a change of location, and you think that this is appropriate, talk to senior staff about this.
4) Encourage the prisoner to keep up their activities, even though they may not feel like doing them. Usually people feel better afterwards if they have forced themselves to go to an evening class, or to play football. Keeping busy also helps to keep one's mind off other worries.
5) Do not tell the prisoner just to snap out of it, or that they are stupid to worry or get depressed over the way things are. You may think that the prisoner is miserable unnecessarily, in which case you might suggest how the situation really is. But it is likely to upset a prisoner further if you tell him that he is stupid to react like that. Instead, show them understanding: there are other ways of looking at the situation.

Suicide attempts

As discussed earlier in Chapter 6, suicide, suicide attempts and self-injury are complicated issues. Always have a second opinion to help determine why the prisoner behaved in that way. Even if you think that the prisoner has hurt him or herself merely to get something out of the prison staff – more attention, a change of location, or some time in hospital – you should ask why they had to resort to self-injury to get it. Often such prisoners have problems which seem impossible to them and their self-injury is the only way out. You may be able to think of another solution. Self-injury should always be taken seriously since it can have a fatal outcome, even though the prisoner did not intend one.

In handling one of these incidents, many of the suggestions that appear in the preceding sections apply here.

1) Show understanding (use listening skills).
2) Try to give hope that there will be a solution.
3) Think of any practical suggestions that might help.
4) Keep the prisoner in contact with staff or other prisoners.
5) Keep the prisoner occupied.

If prisoners feel miserable enough to want to harm themselves, such feelings are likely to seem bigger and more overwhelming if they are left on their own to brood. It is much better to keep them in the company of others where they can have the opportunity to discuss their worries. In some prisons, where there are hospitals, these facilities exist. Elsewhere, staff may just have to make do with existing accommodation.

Keeping prisoners in solitary confinement, particularly where this occurs in a cell stripped of all furniture, reading material, radio etc., is not likely to help anyone's mental state. Someone who is depressed and suicidal should always be under the care of medical staff.

Prisoners with learning difficulties

As we described earlier in the chapter on development, some people may be born with brains that will not develop in the usual way. This disorder may appear in many forms and have several causes. There may be a genetic component which causes a specific type of developmental delay. An example of this is Down's Syndrome. In this case, a child may develop more slowly and have a characteristic appearance. In other cases, there may have been a problem when the baby was still in the womb, or at the time of the baby's birth, which caused general damage to the baby's brain through lack of oxygen. This can cause problems for the growing child which range from just a slight delay in being able to walk and talk etc., or more serious general damage which means that the child has great difficulty coping at school and may need special help.

These are just some examples of learning difficulties that a child can experience and which alter the normal course of development. People may notice that such children are having difficulties, not just at school, but in other areas of life. They may be a bit clumsy or lacking in co-ordination. This is because the brain controls all our movements as well as our thinking capacity. In a few cases, they may also be extremely active or aggressive as their understanding and communication are limited, so that parents are at a loss to know what to do with them. These problems can range from very mild to quite severe, so that the family seeks medical help.

When children with learning difficulties become adults, their problems often increase. This is because we are more tolerant of children behaving unusually, or incompetently, than we are of teenagers or adults. If someone has the physical appearance of an adult, we expect them to behave in a certain fashion. They should be able to read, write, add up, use the telephone, and hold a conversation about the news or what is going on. Someone with even a mild learning difficulty might have problems doing these things. And it is likely to be made more problematic if they are teased, or shouted at, since then they will become flustered and find everything even more difficult. How can you help?

As you may be aware, people with these sorts of difficulties often have a very rough time in prison. They may have difficulty coping on their own outside prison anyway. If you add the further demands of being inside prison, with all the pressure that exists, then they might well be struggling. If you think that a prisoner has a particular learning difficulty, you may find that an assessment is useful. A psychiatrist may be helpful if you are also concerned about a possible mental illness in the prisoner. A clinical psychologist can complete a full assessment of mental ability, as well as the prisoner's ability to cope in everyday activities. Similarly, if you wonder whether it is a reading or writing difficulty, rather than a more general disability, then an educational assessment can pin-point the problems and suggest ways to remedy them. As always, if you are querying any of these possible difficulties, then refer the prisoner to medical staff, who should pursue the problem further.

In dealing with people who may have learning difficulties, there are ways in which you can help to make things easier.

1) Be aware of the prisoner's strengths and weaknesses. This may
    require one of the assessments mentioned above, but can also
    come from your observation of him or her.

2) Try to arrange work or activity into a routine which can be learned and which will not keep changing unpredictably. Some people can take longer to learn a routine, but once it is learned, they can carry it out perfectly well.

3) In teaching a new routine or piece of work, break down the task into stages and teach them one at a time. Only move onto the next stage once the first one has been mastered.

4) Try to use the prisoner's strengths and interests. This is true for all prisoners, but is especially true for those who have difficulties in learning or concentration and may have difficulty adapting to prison life.

5) Try to reduce anxiety. If a mentally handicapped person is being asked to do something that they do not understand, they may be afraid or embarrassed to ask for an explanation. Anxiety may arise so that they become too upset to take anything in. If this happens, try to calm the prisoner (see section on anxiety) in order to explain what you mean.

In making these suggestions, we are aware that they are likely to be difficult to fit into the normal prison regime. It may be that the prison manages such offenders by keeping them in a special group or by transferring them outside prison, to a secure ward in a hospital, for example. Nowadays, hospital treatment is considered inappropriate, unless the individual concerned is suffering from a mental illness at the same time. Learning difficulties, however, do not constitute illness and since mentally handicapped people often have difficulty integrating into communities, isolating them while they are prisoners is unlikely to help them in the long term.

Brain damage

We have described the sort of developmental difficulties that are caused by some problem that occurred at, or before, birth, and which causes the brain to get 'stuck' in its development. But if someone suffers an accident causing damage to the brain, then this can also cause disability.

Examples of such accidents are commonly car crashes in which a driver's head hits the windscreen. If the skull is fractured, then the brain may well be damaged. Even if it is not fractured, the sheer force of the accident may cause the brain to move within the skull and sustain damage. In other cases, violent assaults cause brain injury, through a person falling and hitting the head on a pavement or step, for example, or through receiving a blow to the head. The effects of this damage will depend upon its severity and the part of the brain which has been injured.

There are other ways in which damage can occur. If a person stops breathing for any length of time, the brain may be damaged by being starved of oxygen. Alcohol abuse over a long period of time is also likely to destroy parts of the brain, as is poisoning through different types of noxious gases; for example, car exhaust fumes.

The way that a person is affected by having received an injury to the brain can vary enormously. There may be loss of memory, loss of physical strength or power to one part, or one side, of the body. They may lose very particular abilities, like the ability to understand geographical location, or which is right and which is left. There may also be problems in understanding speech, or in speaking. In other cases the personality can change, so that someone who was understanding and patient suddenly becomes irritable and angry. People with particular head injuries can also lose their inhibitions, so that they start behaving without any care for what others might think or feel. How can you help?

Many of the ways of managing a person with brain damage are similar to those mentioned earlier. A careful assessment and an understanding of a person's strengths and weaknesses should be made in order to decide where best to place them. Allowances might have to be made for what they can and cannot do.

Summary

Although this section has not given details of all the mental illnesses which some people, including prisoners, suffer, it has outlined more common difficulties. It has emphasised the importance of careful assessment, and of describing a prisoner's behaviour clearly. Prison staff are not expected to treat prisoners with psychological problems, but their approach and methods of management will be important in deciding whether a prisoner can cope or not. Suggestions have been made on identifying psychological difficulties and how they can be helped.

Chapter ten

Coping with face-to-face violence

Face-to-face violence is the greatest risk faced by prison staff. In the prison situation, staff are confronted by the aggression of others, aggression which is directed either at themselves or at the prisoners in their care. This can be very stressful. Staff know that physical attacks will occur from time to time but do not know when and where.

In Chapter 5, we explored the nature of aggression: what causes aggression and how we can help people to control their own anger. We learned that violent behaviour is a social interaction. It takes two to make a fight. The way in which you behave can either inflame or defuse the situation. Some prison staff find this hard to accept, but studies show that experienced prison officers are less likely to be assaulted than inexperienced prison officers. Experienced officers have learned how to handle prisoners, they have learned how to defuse tension.

In this chapter, we will look at how to handle face-to-face violence. This can be difficult but as the adage goes, prevention is better (and easier) than cure. We will, therefore, think about how violence can be avoided in the first place, how to prepare oneself, what to do when confronted by violence and how to wind down afterwards. Many of the ideas we talk about are really common sense. It's surprising how uncommon it is to find common sense put into action. You must get into the habit of routinely taking precautions.

Avoiding the problem

If we can make predictions about violent incidents, then we will experience less stress and will be able to react earlier and more effectively.

'But you never know what's going to happen around here, you need a crystal ball. If we knew when someone was going to start a fight, we'd do something about it.'

At first glance, predicting violence would seem to be an impossible task, but from the previous chapter on aggression, we know that aggression does not come out of the blue. There is usually a build-up of anger beforehand. Not only that, but there are certain things either in the environment or between individuals which would make most people angry. We can use all this information to help us avoid the problem of face-to-face violence.

Observe and understand the prisoners in your charge

The experienced officer will tell you that he can sense trouble. We saw in the last two chapters that by observing people and looking for changes in their behaviour you can predict what they are likely to do. This can be used to prevent violence.

For example, if someone is feeling tense, they could be more easily provoked to anger. Everyone feels uptight at some time, particularly if there are problems and no easy or direct way to solve them. Jack has a wife and two children with another baby on the way. When he was taken into custody, he had a job which paid quite well. Now his family have to survive on social security. Right from the start his wife has been having trouble with H.P. payments. Fortunately, Jack's brother, Billy, came back to this country after working abroad. He needed somewhere to stay and was willing to live with the family and pay rent to Jack's wife. It was a relief to know that Billy was there looking after things and helping out with the money. However, recently there has been more trouble with the social security who say that Jack's wife is co-habiting with Billy. Now there are not just the financial worries in Jack's head but also his concerns about what exactly is going on between Billy and his wife. In prison, Jack is powerless to do anything about these personal problems and tends to brood over them; he is tense and worried. Small things are likely to spark off aggression in him. Any comment from another prisoner, whether as a joke or a deliberate attempt to 'wind him up', is likely to cause an assault.

How can we prevent him from being involved in a violent incident? How can we reduce his tension? Is there someone he can see and talk to who can also visit his home? Are they easily and quickly available? Can he communicate directly with his wife in some way? When things are getting on top of him, is there anywhere quiet he can go to calm down?

Does he have access to any activities which would help to distract him, e.g. music, sport, at times when he needs them? Can you use the listening skills that we discussed in Chapter 8 to help him get rid of his worries? By identifying his problem and by trying to resolve it you reduce the chance of him 'acting out' to reduce his tension. This is not being soft. It is a better outcome for the prisoner and for the prison staff.

Motives and emotions of aggressors

If the officer knows the aggressive prisoner well, it may be clear what is making that person angry. If not, it is worth asking others who know him. Understanding the anger could well put you in a better position to deal with it. If someone is violent because he is worried and confused, he needs to be listened to and reassured. If someone is being provoked by another person, he needs to be given a chance to calm down and to get out of the situation for a while. If someone is using violence to get something, his request may be valid even if the way he goes about it is unacceptable.

It is true that restraining a prisoner and removing him from the situation is an effective way to stop the aggression at that time. However, that alone does not deal with why that person was aggressive in the first place and will not prevent him from being aggressive in the future. Furthermore, if other inmates feel that he was unfairly treated, there will be more resentment of staff and other incidents with different prisoners could be more likely in the future.

Not every person is the same and the situations in which people find themselves are also changing. For these reasons each case should be considered on its own merits. We can build up skills in dealing with violence, but we also need to learn where and when each of these skills should be used and match them to each situation we meet.

Taking precautions

In Jack's case it was obvious that he was tense so it should be easy to do something about it. In many cases frustration, anger, jealousy or hatred will not be so obvious so it is important to take precautions just in case. Many of these precautions have to do with the way in which the institution is organised. Many depend on flexibility. Let us consider some examples.

Just as it takes two to tango, you need more than one person to have a violent incident. Except in a very few cases, both people have to play a part in any aggressive outburst. People can 'wind each other up', either deliberately or just because of a 'personality clash'.

If dislikes or personality clashes between two prisoners or between a prisoner and an officer can be identified early on, then aggression can be avoided. You should ask: is the institution flexible enough for prisoners' cells or work-parties to be changed if serious problems arise when two particular individuals are together? Can an officer's role be changed so that he is never in sole charge of a particular inmate who hates him? Are officers on duty in one place regularly enough to know what combinations of people are liable to be troublesome?

Where you talk to a prisoner can be important. You should choose the place carefully. Do not assume that the prisoner's cell is the best place to talk to him. Many prisoners get particularly edgy when staff invade their territory. The way in which a room is furnished can be a hazard. If there is a desk in the room, it is tempting to sit behind it, but think before you do this. Desks are often placed in corners or so that the chair is between the desk and a wall. Is this the situation you would like to be in when faced with a violent person? Far from offering protection, the desk can aid your attacker. It can provide him with something to lean on, to throw on top of you, to stand on or to hide what he is doing. Any objects around the room could be thrown or used as a weapon. Again, we must strike a balance: a completely bare room might be considered to be more safe but could appear more threatening and institutionalised. It may remind the prisoner of an orderly room and make the angry person more tense and more aggressive. Where you choose to sit is also important, putting yourself nearer the door than the other person at least gives you the chance to escape in case of emergency. Remember also to check that the door does not lock behind you when you go into a room with a prisoner.

Institutions often have interview rooms equipped with panic buttons. These can be effective but it is surprising how many of them are sited inappropriately. They are no use if you need to stretch a long way, turn your back to the prisoner or cross to the other side of the room to press them.

If you plan to be on your own with someone who might possibly be aggressive, then it is sensible to let another member of staff know approximately how long you might be so that they can check that you are all right if you overrun your time. Prison officers must be aware of these precautions for themselves but also be aware of them in the protection of civilian staff and visitors. Simple precautions and procedures should be explained and discussed with them to prevent violence from taking place.

Facing aggressive people

There are times when aggression cannot be avoided. You may have to face an angry person. If you know that someone has been aggressive in the past, if they are tense at the moment and 'on a short fuse', if they dislike you or if you have to give them bad news, you may be putting yourself at risk. You must think about precautions to take to protect yourself. Seeing that person on your own may not be advisable but on the other hand, having more than one person around could feel very threatening to the inmate concerned. He might then be put on the defensive and be more likely to act aggressively in order to save face. Indeed, going into an inmate's cell in riot gear may provoke an attack. The decision about how many people should be present must then be taken carefully, weighing up knowledge of the prisoner and of the situation. If, however, you believe that someone might be violent, it would be foolish to go into a situation without having someone nearby to help if necessary. It is usually possible to interview an individual in a room with the door open even slightly so that a call for help could be heard and answered immediately.

Avoid escalation

Your behaviour determines whether the situation escalates or defuses.
    Jim and Ron encounter each other in a pub:

Jim: What do you think you're staring at?
Ron: Just wondering what a girl like her is doing with someone
        like you.
Jim: What's that supposed to mean?
Ron: So you're stupid as well as ugly.

And so it goes on. Each tries to get the better of the other. When one runs out of things to say he will probably resort to physical aggression. Instead of trying to neutralise the situation, each tries to get the better of the other. The more it goes on, the more difficult it becomes for either to back down without losing face. The behaviour of one escalates the behaviour of the other. There is a great danger that you will get sucked in to an upward spiral of aggression that ends in violence. Both our instinctive reactions and our attitudes towards other people can suck us into this spiral. We should examine why.

Instinctive reactions

If someone insults us it is an instinctive reaction to insult them back. If we are hit we may attack that person to make sure that we hurt them enough to stop them from hitting us again. In the prison service these instinctive reactions are not acceptable. They may be considered at best to be unprofessional, at worst to be undue force. Even verbal aggression in self-defence might be frowned upon because it can lead to violence. It is therefore necessary to develop other ways of reacting to neutralise aggression and to calm the situation down rather than 'squaring up' to the other person and probably making things worse. It is important to guard against these instinctive reactions.

Attitudes

Your own attitude towards yourself, prisoners and violent behaviour can affect whether you get into violent confrontation or not. There are no right or wrong attitudes but there are attitudes which are more likely to lead to violence. Have you ever heard a colleague say, '. . . you must never show a trace of fear', 'you should be able to dominate an angry prisoner', 'you can't let them get away with it, if you give an inch they will take a mile'. Attitudes influence behaviour. These attitudes can lead to violence.

If you believe that you can never show you are afraid then you are likely to overcompensate and behave in an aggressive manner – you might shout, glare and make threatening movements towards the angry prisoner. Fear and anxiety are normal responses to violent behaviour so you should not feel ashamed at experiencing them. Letting a prisoner see that you are anxious does not mean he will take control of the situation. If you appear too cool, calm and collected the prisoner may feel that you could not care less. This may further inflame his anger.

The attitude that a real prison officer should be able to dominate every angry prisoner is a common attitude, but an unhelpful one. There will always be occasions where leaving the angry prisoner will actually help him to calm down. If he has just received a 'knock back' for parole and you are the one who wrote part of his parole report, then someone else may have a better chance of calming him down. There will always be times when you need to seek the advice or assistance of others. Other staff may be able to calm the prisoner better than you can.

It is difficult for most of us to shake off the idea that if someone is aggressive towards us, it is a sign of weakness not to stand up to them. Much violence is caused by attempts to save face. It is not true that by backing off you will lose the respect of an angry person. An individual's respect for another person depends on what that person is like and how they handle situations. Losing your temper, for example, is not a way to gain respect. If you cannot control yourself, nobody will believe that you can advise, direct and be in control of others.

Behaviour in the violent situation

When someone is being aggressive, what you say to them is probably less important than how you say it. If a person is really wound up and acting violently, they will probably not be in any state to take in what you are saying. What will make more impression on them is what psychologists call your body language, discussed in Chapter 8.

Think about what people look like when they are being aggressive. They stand directly facing their victim, they go in closer than normal and stare at them, hardly blinking. An aggressive person's body would probably be fairly rigid, perhaps with their fists clenched and their hands on their hips. If you behave like this to an aggressive prisoner, violence is likely to escalate. If that is not the way to behave, how should we behave?

We have already mentioned that staring is a sign of threat or anger, so should be avoided when dealing with aggressive people. But do not go too far the other way. Not looking at the person may also make them think that we are afraid, or not paying attention to them. You should try to keep eye contact as normal as possible: glancing at them, then looking away from their eyes to another part of the face or elsewhere, then back to their eyes.

Posture, too, should seem relaxed. Standing rigid, hands on hips gives the other person the message that you are prepared to take the conflict all the way. On the other hand, hunched shoulders and crossed arms could look as if you expect him to hit you – and might seem like an invitation! In a very tense situation it is difficult to look relaxed but it could have an important influence on how effective we are in handling the situation. Even more important than our posture, as most people are aware, our faces often give away how we are feeling. A clenched jaw, furrowed forehead and knitted eyebrows would probably signal to the other person that you are ready for a fight. But it would also irritate the prisoner if you were grinning. A more appropriate expression might be to look calm, concerned or even worried, depending on the situation and reactions of the other person.

A calm tone of voice might also be appropriate, but again you should always go with the situation. If someone is shouting and very excited or disturbed, you should try to match your tone of voice to his mood. Not going to the same extremes but indicating that you have picked up some of the alarm or urgency that he feels. From there, you can work down to being a little calmer in the hope that he will follow.

What to say

If you say things in the right way, the violent person will gradually be able to take in what you are saying. If you are 'talking someone down', the last thing you want to do is to say something which will annoy them more. Therefore, on no account use insults or sarcasm which will only escalate the aggression.

If the person behaving aggressively feels that someone is trying to understand his point of view, this can have a calming effect. If you can't understand the reason why they are angry you may just have to say something like '. . . I can see that you are angry about something, can you explain to me what it is about?'

Listen to what the prisoner is saying and reflect back what they seem to be saying. 'I see, so you've been waiting three weeks to see the hall governor.' Try to look at the situation from the prisoner's point of view and show them you understand how they feel. 'Yes, I'd get angry if I'd been kept waiting that long and nobody told me why.' Allow them to express these feelings. We all need to ventilate our emotions at times and prisoners are no different in that respect.

To begin with, it is a mistake to reassure or to try to solve problems. Just listen. The angry person needs to be given time to tell you what the problem is and to get over the first wave of emotion. You can say that you will try to help if you can. Try to answer any questions or grievances. A little later, when the person is less aggressive and more able to talk and reason, the specific problems can be addressed. You may then wish to call in other staff (e.g. psychologist, social worker) to help. When people are behaving aggressively, they are often highly emotional and distressed, and may accuse you personally of being responsible for the problems that they are experiencing. With your uniform on you might seem like 'just another officer', so it may be useful to show the prisoner that you are an individual working within the system, not the system itself. There are two ways in which you can do this.

First, you can separate yourself from the organisation, making it clear that you are not responsible for the way the prison runs, e.g. 'I know it seems unfair, but I don't make the rules', 'Sometimes I think it could be done differently, but that's the way the powers that be say it should be done', 'I don't really have any say in that'.

Second, you can give a little personal information so that the prisoner can see you as an individual, e.g. 'I sometimes feel like that', 'Something like that happened to me once; it was awful'.

As the situation begins to get easier, you might want to suggest moving to a more private room to talk. You might offer to get a cup of tea which could help to bring down the emotional level and give you a chance to move the person into a safer environment in case he begins to behave violently again.

Staff issues

When the violence is over and the situation stable, the aggressive incident has probably not been forgotten by the officer or officers involved. They are still left with a variety of feelings: relief but perhaps also guilt about the way they handled things or that they let it occur in the first place. There might be anxiety in case it should happen again, or worry about criticism from others or even the feeling that they have let themselves down.

Of course, if there is physical injury there should be immediate medical attention available. But psychological problems should not be ignored.

After any episode of aggression and violence there should be some sort of 'debriefing' with other officers. This is to look back at the situation and learn from mistakes. The other vital purpose a debriefing serves is to allow officers to talk about how they felt about the incident and to calm themselves down. Those concerned should be alert to point out the things that the staff did correctly.

It may not be advisable for a staff member to return to work immediately following an incident. If preoccupied with the psychological aftermath, they may not be ready to carry on even with normal duties. On the other hand, too lengthy a period away from the establishment might make the officer even more anxious about returning. Again, each situation should be judged on its own merits and on the particular officer concerned.

Specialist psychological counselling may also be provided. It is imperative that this is confidential. If an officer is to be helped, he or she cannot feel that superiors are assessing performance from information given to the counsellor.

Summary

To finish where we began, prevention is better than cure. If officers are trained and prepared to deal with violence, particularly if they have some skills in the psychological techniques mentioned above, aggressive incidents may be diverted before they become too serious. Staff training can also serve to make prison officers feel more competent and less stressed in their work environment.

Chapter eleven

Hostage-taking in prisons

Hostage-taking is one of the most difficult and challenging problems faced by a prison officer, whether he is taken hostage or is just part of the team trying to get the hostage released. Over the last ten years, in our prisons more hostages have been taken than ever before; never before have prison officers been at such risk. Thus, it is important to know what can happen when someone is taken hostage and what we can do to get them released.

In this chapter, we consider the history of hostage-taking and then describe the different approaches which have been used to rescue hostages. We will then look at the pattern of prison incidents over the last decade, where they take place, who is involved, how long it went on, etc. We will then look at what you should do if you are the first person to discover that someone has been taken hostage and what to do if you are unfortunate enough to be taken hostage. Being taken hostage can have a profound effect on the ways in which people feel about themselves and how they cope with everyday life. We finish the chapter by looking at the psychological aftermath of a hostage-taking and describe some of the things that can be done to help the victims.

The history of hostage-taking

Hostage-taking is as old as history, if not older. Paris took Helen – the most beautiful woman in the world – to Troy where she was held hostage for ten years. She was released only after a Greek 'intervention team' managed to trick their way into the city using the Trojan horse. Richard the Lionheart was taken hostage by the King of Austria and the people of England had to pay a large ransom for his return. Hostage-taking used to be legal. In the Middle Ages both national and international laws permitted hostage-taking. People who lent money would sometimes take voluntary hostages to make sure that they got their money back. When countries made international treaties, hostages were sometimes taken to ensure that the treaties would be guaranteed. The Romans used to take hostages from their protectorates to ensure 'good behaviour' and as recently as the Second World War, hostages were taken to keep control over occupied communities.

Since the 1960s, hostage-taking has become a common way of trying to get your own way. It became a favourite method – frequently employed by terrorist groups – to draw attention to their particular cause. In the late 1960s and early 1970s, plane-hijacking seemed to be an everyday occurrence. Terrorists were not the only hostage-takers. People who were caught in criminal acts would sometimes take hostages in a bid to escape from the police. One famous example is the 'Spaghetti House' siege. In 1975 three escaping criminals took six Italian waiters hostage in the basement of a London restaurant. Six days of negotiations followed before they surrendered.

Since the early 1970s hostage-taking has become more common in British prisons. In the late 1980s an incident occurred, on average, every month. Thus, it is more important than ever before that prison officers know how to deal with a hostage-taking.

Methods of resolving hostage-taking

The epidemic of hostage-takings and hijackings which swept the world in the late 1960s was dealt with in different ways. Some ways were more successful than others. The successes and failures of the past can show us how to deal with new hostage incidents. We will now describe the three approaches that have been used, looking at their advantages and disadvantages. The three approaches are: (1) the hard approach, (2) the soft approach, and (3) the softly-softly approach.

The 'hard' approach

The hard approach uses intervention: the place where the hostage is held is stormed and an attempt is made to overcome the hostage-taker and retrieve the hostage. This is often a popular approach with prison staff and also with the general public. The problem is dealt with quickly, proper control is regained by the authorities, retribution is swift and potential hostage-takers are deterred. Unfortunately, it is a high risk strategy. The hostage will probably get injured or killed. Experience shows that intervention is very dangerous for the hostage. One study of the hard approach used against terrorists showed that four times as many people were killed during the assaults by the authorities than were 'executed in cold blood'. One famous example is the take-over of Attica Prison in 1972. The National Guard stormed the prison and in the mêlée, fifteen hostages were killed by shooting. When the bullets were recovered from the bodies it was clear that they had been fired by the National Guard not by the perpetrators.

The hard approach has had its successes. In 1976, Palestinian terrorists hijacked a plane containing many Israeli passengers to Entebbe in Uganda. Israeli forces intervened and freed the hostages. Another dramatic example was the storming, in 1980, of the Iranian embassy in London by members of the Special Air Service. This was a success in that all the hostages were released unharmed, although some of the perpetrators were killed. Two points should be noted about these successes. First, the intervention teams were highly trained and highly skilled. Second, intervention was only used when it was clear that negotiation would not work. Because of the dangers of intervention, it must always be the last option when prisoners take hostages.

The 'soft' approach

With the soft approach you give in to the demands of the perpetrator. You do what he wants. The soft approach has the advantage that you get the problem over with quickly; you get the hostage back before he gets harmed. Unfortunately, if you use the soft approach, if you give in to demands, you will probably end up with an epidemic of hostage-takings. Prisoners will learn that taking a hostage gets them what they want. Not only will there be more hostage-takings but also demands will start to escalate. Perpetrators will want more in return for the hostage. This weakness in the soft approach is obvious if we look at what happened in Brazil in 1969 and 1970. In September 1969 Brazilian terrorists kidnapped the American Ambassador and demanded the release of fifteen terrorists. Their demand was granted. Eight months later they demanded the release of forty terrorists for the release of the German Ambassador. This demand was also granted. Six months later they demanded and obtained the release of seventy terrorists in return for the release of the Swiss Ambassador. It is clear that with the soft approach, demands increase and come more frequently. Another approach is required.

The 'softly-softly' approach

The failure of both the hard approach and the soft approach showed that another strategy was needed. In the early 1970s, it became clear that a middle path might be effective. This was the softly-softly approach. In the softly-softly approach the authorities play for time – this allows anger and frustration to diffuse – they make no concessions but pursue the release of the hostage through negotiation. The theory was worked out at Scotland Yard but it was the New York Police Department who first showed how effective the approach could be. They showed that if they stood firm and reassured the perpetrator that they were not going to intervene, then their negotiators could get to work. The negotiators would calm down the perpetrator then gradually build up a relationship and gain control before persuading the perpetrator that he should release the hostage. Hostage-taking is frequent in New York and thus it did not take long for the Department to demonstrate that this approach was extremely successful.

The softly-softly method worked with terrorists as well as criminals. A striking example of its use was when Dr Tiede Herrema was taken hostage by the IRA. Dr Herrema was held for eighteen days while the authorities negotiated with his IRA captors. The first demand for the release of three IRA prisoners was gently, but firmly, refused. The second demand for the release of one prisoner was treated in the same way. The captors changed tack; they asked for a ransom of £3 million. After prolonged negotiations this demand was also refused. Talking continued until after eighteen days Dr Herrema was released without any concessions being made.

The softly-softly approach is the most successful strategy in most cases. Playing for time allows the perpetrator to calm down and begin to appreciate the futility of his position. Make no mistake, it is not an easy approach. Negotiation may take a long time, there will be pressure from the public, the press and the politicians to 'do something', to rescue the victim. There is no easy solution to a hostage incident: the softly-softly approach is the best approach we have.

Hostage-taking in British prisons

We have talked mostly about terrorist and criminal hostage-taking. We will now focus on what happens when prisoners take people hostage.

In the last decade we have built up a lot of experience in British prisons and some patterns of hostage-taking are becoming apparent. Let us examine these. Most incidents take place in cells. This has the advantage that it is easy to control but it is usually difficult to intervene if and when intervention becomes necessary. Prisoners prefer to use prison officers rather than fellow prisoners as hostages because they believe that this gives them more bargaining power. Various weapons have been used including knifes, razors and a dummy gun. Fortunately, although weapons have been used, physical injuries to hostages are relatively rare and tend to be slight. Most incidents tend to be fairly brief, lasting under five hours. However, this is not always the case. Recent Scottish incidents have lasted several days.

Who takes hostages and why do they do it? These are important questions to which we still do not have full answers. Studies have failed to find a typical 'hostage-taker'. The best evidence we have is that they tend to have a history of violence, they are usually serving a sentence of more than five years and they are often under twenty-five years old.

When we move from looking at who takes hostages to why people take hostages we have even less information. The best information we have indicates that most incidents occur on the 'spur of the moment'; they are not planned but are often a way of coping with unpleasant experiences such as a 'dear John' letter, getting a 'knock back' or being badly treated. There is also a 'copy-cat' process. When one prisoner takes a hostage, others think of it as a way of making a protest or expressing concern. Because we cannot give general guidelines about which prisoners are likely to take a hostage, the gallery officer must always be alert to the possibility and be aware of the mood, thoughts and concerns of prisoners around him. The gallery officer must keep in touch with the bush telegraph.

Coping with hostage-taking – first on the scene

If the bush telegraph fails and you see someone being taken hostage, what should you do? The person who is 'first on the scene' has an important job to do; the skill with which they do this job can either help or hinder the release of the hostage.

If you are on the scene when the hostage is taken, your first reaction might be to intervene. You may have to make a split second decision, but the golden rule is don't intervene if this will threaten the hostage. If in doubt, do not intervene. Make sure you are not taken as an extra hostage. Extra hostages give the perpetrators extra power. Your primary task is to report what has happened quietly, calmly and accurately. Do not set off the alarm because this will probably 'wind up' the perpetrator. If the bell does not make him more uptight, the arrival of reinforcements certainly will.

The 'first on the scene' should never start negotiating. Never make commitments to the perpetrator. For example, never say, 'I'll go and get the governor', or 'I'll try to arrange your visit' or 'you can have my car to drive away in'. Do not agree to anything. Do not be specific; for example, do not say, 'I'll get the P.O. along in five minutes'. Rather, give vague assurances, e.g. 'I'll get someone along to talk to you soon'. If the 'first on the scene' makes promises to the perpetrator then this gives the negotiators great difficulties because they cannot agree to such promises. This may enrage the perpetrator: the hostage may be harmed.

It is important that you give your superiors accurate information about what is happening. Invaluable information would include how many hostages and how many perpetrators there are, who they are and where they are located. Have they built a barricade and what sort of weapons do they have? When you report back, if you do not know something admit that you do not know. This helps to reduce confusion.

Coping with hostage-taking – being a hostage

If you are unfortunate enough to be taken hostage, what should you do to reduce the danger you are in? People who have thought about being taken hostage and are partly prepared for it seem to cope with the experience with much less distress than those who do not expect it. We will try to help you to prepare just in case.

Before we think about how a hostage should behave, however, we should consider how the perpetrator is behaving and what he is experiencing. It is obvious that a hostage incident is a stressful experience for the hostage; perhaps less obviously, it is also stressful for the perpetrator. In the early stages of an incident the perpetrator may appear disturbed; he may get very excited and feel great power. He has gone from being a prisoner with little control over his life to someone who thinks he can get anything he wants by threatening his hostage. The perpetrator may feel stressed, particularly if he has taken a hostage on an impulse. He may look strange. He may be hyper-aroused, that is, he may start breathing quickly, his pupils may dilate, he may seem confused and distracted – starting at any strange sounds – and he may behave irrationally. In extreme cases, perpetrators have been known to vomit and lose control of their bowels. They are not mentally ill but just displaying the effects of extreme stress.

As the incident progresses the perpetrator will begin to calm down. A person can only stay highly aroused for short periods. As the futility of his situation becomes more apparent he may become depressed and withdrawn.

If you are a hostage how do you handle this high emotion and these changes in mood? When a prisoner is uptight it is important to do nothing which might provoke him. You must keep your feelings of anger under control and not show your hostility. You should co-operate with him and talk to him. Do not refuse to talk to him. Talking is your most powerful weapon. By talking you can help to calm him down, you can get him to see you as a person and not an object to be bartered or hurt so that he can achieve his goals. You can build rapport by showing and saying that you understand what is upsetting him: 'yes, the food is lousy in here', 'it's about time they got these visits sorted out', 'yes, the governor is a right bastard'. Where possible, you should 'self-disclose', that is, tell him something about yourself. For example, if he starts talking about his wife and family try to mention yours. This helps to develop rapport. It makes him see you as more human. It gives you greater safety.

You may be tempted to try to overcome the perpetrator. You should not attempt this as if you are unsuccessful he is likely to damage you. It may seem cowardly not to act but if you enrage the perpetrator you help neither yourself nor the negotiators.

If the problem drags on, you might find that your concentration and your morale begin to drop. Try to sustain both. If the situation allows, eat and sleep when you can.

Morale is harder to maintain. Remind yourself that most incidents are resolved by talking. Experience shows that the longer the incident goes on the less likely you are to be injured. There will be an experienced and well-trained team working to get you out and people will be looking after your family. Maintain your morale by maintaining your professional role. As a hostage you can help to bring the perpetrator down and thereby help end the incident. In the South Malacan train siege, a journalist, who was taken hostage, behaved as if he was covering the story, writing down the details of what was happening and talking to the other hostages. He was able to sustain his morale and his attention by sticking to his professional role. A prison officer can do the same, by doing what we have suggested above.

You can maintain your morale in other ways; for example, if there are several hostages and you are allowed to talk to each other. Do talk, do not avoid talking about personal feelings and experiences and try to listen to the fears and worries of the others. When people are experiencing extreme stress, support from other people is important. In the South Malacan train siege fellow hostages supported each other and kept morale up.

Being a hostage is a stressful experience and can produce some unusual psychological effects. Not every hostage has these experiences – it depends on your past experience and how long and in what way you are held hostage. However, it is important that you know what might happen as it is less disturbing if it does occur.

Perhaps the most common and understandable feelings experienced by a hostage are fear and helplessness. The fear might be the strongest you have ever experienced – the fear for your very life. Many hostages feel totally helpless, imagining that they cannot affect this all-powerful perpetrator. As we have seen that is not the case. You can have an effect – you can influence the situation so that he calms down.

These are obvious psychological effects but other less obvious things might happen. Time may become distorted. If the perpetrator is making a deadline – saying he will harm you if something is not done in thirty minutes – time may fly. At other periods, time may seem to be slowed down. Some hostages have 'out of the body' experiences. For example, they might feel they are floating above the cell watching what is going on down below. This is a form of 'depersonalisation' which can happen in all sorts of stressful situations. Do not worry about it; you are not going mad. Sometimes a hostage may experience hallucinations. Hostages who have been restrained, isolated and blindfolded have reported seeing things. This is caused by a combination of stress and lack of visual stimulation. For example, single-handed yachtsmen, who get exhausted travelling great distances with only the sea to look at, often report such hallucinations. The hallucinations go away when the stress goes away.

Before concluding this section, we should consider one final effect of being a hostage: the 'Stockholm Effect'. Sometimes when a hostage is held for some time they begin to have strong positive feelings for the perpetrator and their cause or grievance. It is odd that a hostage could feel good about someone who is threatening to kill or maim them. But it does happen. Perhaps the most famous example is that of Patty Hearst. She was kidnapped by the Symbionese Liberation Army and in the end she became an active member. Patty Hearst was not an isolated case. At the Iranian embassy siege, one of the hostages told her rescuers that her captor was 'a nice boy'.

Hand in hand with this positive feeling for the perpetrator goes a negative feeling for the authorities – 'why don't they give him what he wants?', 'they're forcing him to hurt me because they are being so stupid'. We are not sure why the Stockholm Effect happens. One explanation is that after a while the hostage is grateful that the all-powerful perpetrator has not taken his life. The perpetrator gives life by the act of not taking it away.

Coping with hostage-taking – the aftermath

The release of the hostage is not always the end of his problems. Many hostages suffer long-term psychological changes. This can happen even if the hostage incident has been brief: the intensity, not the duration, of the incident is important. Some of the problems are predictable. Many hostages report nightmares – or even frightening day-dreams – about what happened to them when they were taken hostage. Phobias are common. One third of the Dutch hostages who were captured in the South Malacan train siege developed phobias of trains. They could not bring themselves to get on trains. Many prison officers find it difficult to go back into the jail or cell block where the incident occurred. Often they feel they are being watched and threatened – they jump at the slightest sound – they are scared that it is going to happen again. Anxiety can come out in other ways. One ex-hostage had locks fitted to all the doors of his house – internal and external doors – and then he went around locking them behind him. In the short term, this kept his anxiety under control; in the long term his anxiety and family problems took over.

Some of the changes are less obvious. Many hostages become acutely aware of how vulnerable they are, feeling that their lives could end at any time. Even people who have had a lot of interests in their lives lose their interests, they do not get pleasure from anything anymore and they come to believe that their lives have been wasted. They feel useless, worthless and a failure. The picture is often one of depression, despair and apathy.

Guilt is another common feeling. A hostage may feel guilty at what he did or did not do during the incident. Some may feel ashamed that they did not take their captor on, they did not 'have a go'. Some may feel ashamed that they broke down and cried or even begged their captor for mercy. The thought of facing work mates who know these things can terrify and cause shame. These fears may not be without foundation. Some hostages become stigmatised by their work mates and are forced – directly or indirectly – to give up their job.

Being taken hostage is a terrifying experience. It can change how a person feels and behaves drastically. What should you do if it happens to you? There are a few guidelines which you should follow. If you get any of the feelings or worries we have described, tell someone. Don't cover up. Don't be a John Wayne. Either tell a welfare officer or go to your general practitioner. Ask to be referred to someone who specialises in treating anxiety problems. Get the welfare officer or G.P. to refer you to a clinical psychologist. The clinical psychologist will help you in several ways. First, he or she will help you talk about your worries and fears in a safe and confidential setting. Second, he or she will be able to show you that you are not the first person to feel this way and that your response is 'normal' to this type of experience. Third, he or she will be able to teach you how to control the thoughts which make you feel sad and frightened, how to reduce the feelings of tension, how to tackle any phobias and how to improve your sleep. It is important that hostages get professional help otherwise fears can 'incubate' and the hostages can grow more and more distressed.

The hostage may not be the only victim; wives and families of the hostage also suffer. In some ways, a hostage-taking can be harder for the wife and family of the hostage than it is for the hostage. Being remote, the family always fears the worst. Frequently, these victims will need at least as much professional help as the primary victim.

Coping with hostage-taking – other staff

If a hostage incident is going on in your prison and you are not directly involved, you may still have an important role to play. The prison organisation will be stretched and strained, other prisoners may be uptight, ready to join in to support their fellow prisoners. It is important that you carry on with your work in a calm and low-key manner. Reassure prisoners and do nothing to wind them up. A second incident is the last thing which is needed.

You may be tempted to go and see what is going on – don't. Avoid the 'pit-head' syndrome. Spectators can inflame the incident or set negotiations back hours or days. In one incident, prison officers who set out to see what was going on 'wound up' perpetrators by blundering through a door when the perpetrators did not expect them. Keep your curiosity under control.

Staff will be drafted in to do the many tasks involved in sorting out a hostage incident. You may be required to do extra duties to cover. You will also be required to do what you are told without question. The complexity of any hostage problem, and the speed with which it may change, require everyone involved to respond to commands. Lack of discipline can harm the hostage.

There are certain people you should talk to and certain people you should not talk to. Talk to your family; explain to them what is happening and explain that you are not at risk. Families worry because they fear the worst and these fears are often fed by the press and television coverage of the incident. Do not talk to the media. Reporters may pester you as you leave the establishment. Their interests are not always the same as the interests of the hostage. In one incident, a press helicopter repeatedly flew over an incident despite repeated requests to stop. The perpetrators shifted from being quite calm and amenable to being very hostile and aggressive – they thought the SAS were coming. Perpetrators often have access to radios and they may monitor the coverage that they are getting. Bad coverage can 'wind them up'. Other coverage may reveal plans or sensitive information. You should not talk to reporters; they will get the information they need from official sources.

Summary

Hostage-taking used to be a technique employed by nations to enforce their will. In the 1960s and 1970s terrorists adopted hostage-taking as a way of making demands and drawing national and international attention to their causes. Prisoners in the United States and more recently in the United Kingdom have adopted hostage-taking as a way of relieving tension or making demands. It is a problem which is here to stay. Having read this far, we hope you are better prepared to face an incident should it occur in your prison.

Chapter twelve

Stress and working in prisons

Bill was a Principal Officer with twenty years' experience. He was moved to a wing containing twenty-five argumentative, unpredictable and dangerous prisoners – prisoners with a history of violence. He continued to work well, he adopted a tough attitude and controlled the wing with a 'rod of iron'. The wing governor was impressed by his performance.

At home his family noticed a difference. Bill became irritable – his wife and children could never do anything properly. He spent long hours in the local social club by himself, drinking and smoking. He sometimes drank a few pints before going on duty. After six months he began feeling dizzy and faint. He went to his doctor and found that his blood pressure was high and he was given treatment for this.

Another officer, Gerry, was a basic grade officer. He was taken hostage by three inmates and held for twenty-six hours. The inmates had knives and threatened to cut him up and kill him. The inmates were tense and uptight; one of them was almost out of control. Gerry feared that this inmate would go berserk and kill him. Senior staff negotiated him out of the cell and he was told to go home, take a few days off and put his feet up. Gerry went home but could not sleep. His muscles were tense, he could not sit still and had to pace up and down. His wife tried to talk to him but he just shouted back at her.

After three days he went back to work. As he got nearer the prison his heart started to beat faster, he sweated and he felt sick. He got to the muster room but he still felt uncomfortable because his friends seemed to be keeping their distance. Gradually, over the next few days, going into the prison became harder and harder. He could not get up in the morning, he felt very sorry for himself and he could not see any future. He began to cry at times and he lost his appetite. He did not want anything to do with his family or friends - he would lie all day in a darkened room. Hopelessness overwhelmed Gerry and he swallowed his wife's sleeping pills. Fortunately his wife found him in time and got him to hospital.

Both Bill and Gerry suffered the effects of stress. Bill's stress was long-term stress because he had to cope with a difficult wing over a six-month period. Gerry's stress was a 'one off' catastrophe. We all experience stress, both the day-to-day hassles and problems, and also major catastrophes in our lives. The cases of Bill and Gerry show that stress can affect us in many ways; it affects us physically and psychologically, influencing our lives at work and at home.

In this chapter, we will look at the ways in which stress can affect people. We will describe the things which make prisons stressful places to work in and will conclude by making suggestions about ways of coping with stress.

The effects of stress

The effects of stress are widespread and have an influence on many areas of our lives. Stress can lead to physical and psychological illness, problems at work, disturbance in our families and social lives, addiction and perhaps even criminal behaviour.

Psychological disturbance

There is a mass of scientific evidence which shows that stressful experiences lead to psychological disturbance. It is common sense. If many bad things happen to you then you are going to get upset by this. The effects can be profound and serious. Stressful experiences have been shown to cause anxiety, depression, mental illness and suicidal behaviour. Depression and anxiety are the most common effects. When someone is depressed, he or she will experience sadness, tearfulness, irritability, concern about him or herself, the world and the future. In addition, that person may have suicidal ideas, their sleep may be disturbed, their weight may drop and concentration may be poor. In a study in Glasgow, 37 per cent of cases of depression found in the general population were caused by stress.

Anxiety is another common result of stressful experiences. People who are anxious may experience considerable physical tension. Their sleep may be disturbed, they may worry and their concentration may be disturbed. They may be fearful of entering particular situations such as going into work. In a study in London, 72 per cent of cases of anxiety were caused by stress. It is clear, therefore, that stress can have a significant impact on people's psychological well-being.

Less commonly, and only in vulnerable people, stress may bring on acute mental breakdowns. In other cases, stressful experiences or chronic stress may lead people to attempt to take their own lives. Indeed, recent studies in Edinburgh show a high association between the stress of being unemployed and suicide attempts.

Physical illness and disturbance

Most people would agree that stressful experiences can lead people to be anxious and depressed. However, there is evidence which shows that stressful experiences can lead to both minor and major physical disturbance. At the minor level, stress may lead to fatigue, headaches, impaired concentration (which may lead to accidents), sleep disturbance, indigestion and, perhaps surprisingly, the common cold. Stress may also lead to more serious and profound physical problems. These problems range from skin problems through high blood pressure and coronary heart disease to sexual difficulties, peptic ulcers and inflammation of the appendix. The effects of stress can be powerful. For example, recent evidence suggests that 34 per cent of cases of inflamed appendices may be caused by stress.

Family and social disturbance

Stressful experiences can lead, either directly or indirectly, to significant family and social problems. Someone under stress may become irritable and tense. This may cause more arguments at home and lead to long-standing marital conflicts. If someone becomes over-anxious and tense, he may avoid friends and colleagues; he will often stop going to his social club or going to see friends.

Addiction

Stress may lead to addiction. By addiction is meant an over-dependence on food, alcohol, drugs (legal or illicit) or nicotine. Some people who are under stress find that they feel better if they eat, drink, smoke or use drugs. If such activities continue for a long time, it is possible to become addicted to these substances. Alcohol, and those drugs which get rid of the feeling of tension, are perhaps the most addictive. These addictions result in their own health and social problems.

Criminal behaviour

Stressful experiences may lead people to commit certain forms of criminal acts. The most common example quoted is the case of shoplifting. The evidence is not overwhelming but stress may be a factor in some cases.

Difficulties at work

Stress in the home and stress in the work-place can lead to difficulties at work. In a study of prison officers in New Jersey, it was discovered that three major types of problem emerged at work. First, officers who were experiencing stress were often absent from work for short periods. They avoided going into their prison because of stress. Second, officers reverted to the traditional custodial role and failed to carry out the welfare duties which are an integral part of the activities of prison officers. Third, the concentration of officers was poorer and they were less able to cope quickly when difficult situations developed.

Other things which can happen are that officers can become argumentative and callous or apathetic and withdrawn. These difficulties can generate further problems.

Why are prisons stressful places?

The first question to ask is, 'are prisons stressful places to work in?' If you ask some officers they will tell you that they do not suffer from stress but all their work-mates do. The Americans call this the 'John Wayne Syndrome'. What do the statistics say? The evidence is not very conclusive, but mortality statistics show that prison officers have a higher risk of heart disease than the general population. This may well be because of stress although it may also be related to habits of smoking, drinking or overeating.

Evidence from studies of American prison officers is more convincing. All entrants to the prison service are screened for good health when they first join, yet the rates of stomach problems, skin complaints, low back pain and high blood pressure while in service are higher than in the general population. Also, the rate of minor psychological problems seems to be high in these officers.

The rate of stress disorders does appear to be higher in prison employees. Why is this the case? There are probably three reasons. Let us look at each of these in turn.

Nature of the job

Prison officers may have to deal with difficult and disturbed individuals whose behaviour is, at times, unpredictable. The officer must be vigilant and is often required to move from little to high activity at a moment's notice. Unpredictability can be stressful, as can be the continued hostility of inmates. In certain establishments officers may feel physically vulnerable and continued alertness to attacks may be stressful. The fact that the amount of sick leave is generally higher in maximum security prisons would tend to confirm this view.

On a more general level the lack of stimulation or challenge in many prison officers' jobs can be distressing.

Role in the organisation

An officer's position and function in the prison service can affect the nature and extent of stress with which he is confronted: the stresses on a governor are different from those on a basic grade officer. Studies suggest that problems of 'role' in the organisation are regarded as more important by officers than are problems with prisoners. What are these problems? A common complaint, at all levels, is that there is poor communication from above. Orders, policies and procedures are changed but these changes are not communicated. Where such a situation exists, stress exists because of uncertainty. A further source of dissatisfaction, and perhaps stress, arises when people feel they cannot affect decisions taken. The majority of prison officers can have little impact on policies. This can generate resentment as they often feel they know the prisoners better than the decision-makers. Studies of decision-making in other work-places show that lack of involvement in decision-making can be highly stressful.

A final aspect of the prison officer's job which may make it stressful is the ambiguity of the job. The prison officer's job involves concern for security and concern for the welfare of prisoners. These roles can be incompatible; understanding an individual's problem, yet having to lock him up, can cause conflicts. This problem is made more intense when there is little training for 'the welfare role'.

Prisons and the outside world

Society can have a negative view of the prison officer. Friends and neighbours often do not appreciate the difficulties of the job. The officer or his family may be given the cold shoulder in the neighbourhood. A further difficulty may be the fear of physical abuse by ex-prisoners on the officer or his family.

These are some of the factors which make prisons stressful places to work in. We will now describe ways of coping with stress.

The need for an optimum level of pressure

Not all pressure is bad. Some pressure is desirable. Indeed, being under-stretched can be as bad as being over-stressed. It has been established that each individual has a particular level of pressure at which he or she can best operate. This is determined by a variety of factors including experience, personality and the level of support from friends, colleagues and family. If you go away for a quiet holiday you might well have no pressure on you at all, and this is regarded as being desirable. If your employer decides to put you on permanent holiday, and makes you unemployed, the pressure of work would be removed, but this would be most undesirable, because other pressures arise – 'How do I pay the mortgage?' 'Where do I find another job?' On the other hand, if you take on a new job which has a variety of major responsibilities, you may feel under pressure, but because the work is interesting and exciting and you feel you can do it, you might enjoy the pressure. Stress occurs when you feel that many demands are being made on you, and you begin to doubt that you can cope. It is being under pressure, and worrying that you may not manage all that has to be done. If you are stressed, you may become anxious, irritable and aggressive. You can cope with more pressure if it is desirable, less if it is undesirable. Let us consider some of the techniques for coping with stress.

Coping with stress

There are two broad ways to deal with stress. These are 'stress prevention' and 'stress management'. By 'stress prevention', we mean organising your life in such a way that you have enough, but not too much, stress. By 'stress management', we mean the techniques which you can use to reduce the effects of stress when you are exposed to stressful experiences. Some of the techniques will work for some people and not for others. A variety of techniques will be described and there should be some which will help you prevent or manage the stress which you experience. There is a certain degree of overlap between strategies for 'stress prevention' and strategies for 'stress management'. However, it is probably clearer to have them divided in this way.

Strategies for stress prevention

Understand the nature of stress

We saw above that each person needs a balanced amount of pressure. It is important, therefore, to work out what suits you best and recognise the experiences which you find difficult to cope with. Some people may be able to cope with difficult prisoners but find it hard to tell a subordinate that he is not doing his job properly. In addition, it is important to remember to identify the early signs that you are becoming stressed. The signs of stress and the causes of stress were described above. You should consider to what extent any of these may apply to you.

Keep physically fit

Steady exercise can remove some of the harmful stress hormones from the body. In addition, the feelings of anxiety and depression can be alleviated by exercise. Perhaps more importantly, from the point of view of prevention, keeping fit makes people better able to withstand those stresses which occur. The body is more able to cope with any harmful effects that it experiences.

Analyse situations with which you have coped

There will be times when you cope successfully with stressful situations. After this happens, work out what you did which was helpful and what you did which was unhelpful. If you had a heated argument with one of the inmates, you may have gone home and shouted at the children. On another occasion you may have gone and walked the dog, played football or helped a friend with decorating. Work out which of these strategies was most effective and next time try to do that again when the situation arises.

Realise that you cannot do everything

There will be times with the family, the job and your social life where things get on top of you because you do not have enough time to do everything. When this happens you have to work out what your prior-ities are, and if necessary pay someone to do the time-consuming task you do not really have time for.

Minimise problems in your life by changing your views of them

The Greeks thought that 'men are disturbed not by things but by the views which they take of them'. In other words, it is not the stresses or hassles which actually upset us but how we think about these and how we interpret them. If you can find situations in your life that make you feel uptight or stressed, then you may be able to change these by changing the way in which you interpret the situation. For example, if you are compulsive about being on time for everything, then this may make you uptight when you are running behind your schedule. You must ask yourself if it is worth it; ask yourself the question, 'What is the worst thing that can happen if I am late?' You will usually find that by talking to yourself in an objective or positive way, you can reduce this stress in your life.

Develop an effective support system

One of the most positive results which has come out of the research on stress is that having support from your family, your friends and your colleagues is of considerable importance. The prison service is a close-knit group and can provide support to its members. It probably sounds very easy to say so, but one of the most effective ways of dealing with stress is to find someone to confide in about your problems. The opportunity of expressing your feelings about a problem appears to reduce the feelings of stress. It is important to pick the right kind of person. You have to trust the person and be sure that they will not reveal your confidences. You have to feel that they understand what you are talking about. You have to have respect for them. If you have such a person available, talking to them can be a very effective way of dealing with stress. Such a person may be found among your friends, your colleagues or your family. In addition, professional support may be provided at times of extreme need by a clergyman or general practitioner or by a psychiatrist or psychologist in the prison service.

The above are some of the strategies for preventing stress and they overlap with techniques for managing stress.

Skills for managing stress

If you fail to prevent stress then you need to find techniques to manage the stress you have. Some of the following techniques may be useful.

Relaxation training

When we are under stress we become tense and experience a variety of bodily symptoms. These bodily symptoms might include fast heartbeat, higher rate of breathing, sweating and butterflies in the stomach. All these feelings are caused by the adrenalin in our bodies. We can control these feelings by using relaxation techniques. There are three broad types of technique: (1) muscle relaxation, (2) deep breathing, and (3) imagining non-stressful situations.

Muscle relaxation

Muscle relaxation can be carried out either lying down or whilst sitting in a comfortable chair. It is a skill and, like any other skill, requires practice to acquire competence. The overall aim is to become aware of when your muscles are tense and learn how to relax. Start by clenching your fists tightly. Feel the tension in your fists, feel the tension in your wrists until it is almost sore and then relax. Notice the difference between the tension in your arms and in your fists when you are tense and when you relax. Do this again, clenching your fists so that your arms become tight. Hold them tight for five seconds and then relax for more than five seconds. You should go through this procedure of tensing the muscles, holding them tense for five seconds and then relaxing them, with all the major muscle groups in your body. These might include the following:

1) hands
2) forearms
3) biceps

4) forehead
5) the muscles round your eyes and nose
6) cheeks and jaw muscles
7) neck and shoulders
8) stomach muscles
9) calf muscles
10) thigh muscles

You can go through this procedure in any order which you find accept-able. With practice, you will find that you can remove most of the physical tension from the body and feel both physically and mentally relaxed. Audio-tapes of relaxation techniques are available and they often prove useful.

Deep breathing

When we are under stress, our breathing pattern changes; we tend to breathe more quickly and more shallowly. This tendency is more pro-nounced in some people than others. For those people who do breathe in a shallow and fast manner, when they are under stress, the breathing makes their bodily symptoms worse. Many of the symptoms we mentioned above, including rapid heartbeat, sweating, dryness of the mouth and shaking, can be caused by shallow and rapid breathing. If you are feeling under stress then deep breathing may reduce this feeling. Once again, like physical relaxation, this technique takes practice. You should practise this technique when you are not under stress so that you are skilled enough to use it when stressful experiences come along. You should try the following practice exercise. Sit comfortably with your eyes closed. Put your hands just below your stomach and breathe in deeply. Breathe using your abdomen rather than your chest. If you are breathing deeply then your hands should move out when you are breathing in. Hold the breath and count up to five. Then let the breath out slowly and in a controlled fashion and count to five once more. Repeat this five or six times and you will usually find that you are more relaxed. If you find that you are not breathing deeply, i.e. your hands are not moving out when you are breathing in, then you should concentrate on getting movement in your abdomen before you concentrate on holding your breath for a long time.

Imagining positive situations

Some people react to stress in a physical way while others react to stress in a psychological way. Indeed, some unfortunate people react in both ways. It is important, therefore, to learn how to cope with distressing feelings and thoughts. One technique is to learn to imagine positive situations. We all have thoughts and images coming into our minds. If these thoughts and images are negative then they will affect how we feel psychologically and how we feel physically. We have control over these thoughts and images; however, many of us do not exercise this control as effectively as we should. Once again it is a skill which needs to be practised and developed. This skill can be practised while sitting quietly in a chair. You should think about a situation or experience from your past which has made you feel happy and relaxed. You should focus on this in your mind and try to remember every detail of where you were, what happened, how you felt. While you are doing this other thoughts, perhaps negative thoughts, will try to intrude. You must push these out of the way and concentrate on the detail of the positive situation which you have enjoyed and which has made you feel relaxed. You should try to get as clear, bright and colourful an image as you can. The image should be as detailed as possible. This sort of skill is quite difficult to acquire and requires a lot of concentration; however, with practice, you will find that it enables you to cut out much of the 'jumble of thoughts' which may go on in your head.

Practise worry control

One of the greatest problems is failing to leave your troubles at work. By worry control, we mean turning off worries and concentrating on something else. Many people find this difficult while others do it quite naturally. If you are one of the people who find this difficult, then it is important to identify things which help you to cut off your worries. It may be that using positive images, like those we mentioned above, will help you to cut off worries. It may be that getting involved in your hobbies or with other people can distract you from your worries.

Catastrophes

When we are worrying about something we often let the thoughts go round and round in our head and illogical ideas develop. It is important, therefore, to work out likely consequences of what we are worried about. One way of doing this is to try to work out the worst possible thing that could happen. In other words, work out the catastrophe that would happen if your worst fears came to pass. It is often not as bad as you had thought. By working out the worst consequences of our worry we can often get things into proper perspective and thus reduce the stress.

Learn to use leisure activities to counteract stress

We saw above that some people react to stress in a psychological way while others react in a physical way. It is important to work out how you react and work out strategies which help you to counteract this. If a stressful experience makes you feel that you cannot concentrate on anything and that you are worrying, then perhaps the best stress reliever is an activity which distracts your thoughts. Such activities might be reading a book, playing chess, playing snooker, doing a crossword puzzle, talking to your friend – anything which distracts you from your thoughts. If, in contrast, you react to stress in a physical way and you feel uptight, jittery and tense, then physical activity might be a means of reducing your stress. In that case you might want to go and play football, go for a long swim, have a walk in the hills, play golf or go for a run. You have to learn which activities work for you, which activities reduce your stress.

Use constructive self-talk

When most of us are under stress we tend to have a lot of thoughts, pictures and sensations going through our heads. If we are feeling worried and uptight, then these thoughts, pictures and sensations will be negative in quality. We may worry about ourselves, about our future and about our world. Common negative thoughts would be, 'I'm useless at this job, I'll never get the work done on time' or, 'there is no way I'm going to get promotion'. If you are feeling under stress and rather depressed then it is important to use positive self-talk. Self-talk is just what it says, talking to yourself, not out loud but in your mind. Positive self-talk can be used in different situations to help us cope with stressful experiences. These would include 1) before going into a stressful experience, 2) when it is happening, 3) when you are really feeling uptight and things seem to be getting out of control, 4) after it happens.

1) Suppose you have to go to a promotion board. Before you go into the board you can say the following things:

a) 'A good thing to do is to stay calm and practise what I am going to say.'
b) 'I know my job and I stand a fair chance of getting promoted.'
c) 'My job in the interview is to put myself across in the most positive way.'

2) When you go into the board you can sit down and think to yourself:
   a) 'Keep calm, I've been through boards before, no problem.'
   b) 'I'm in control of myself, it will be all right, just listen to what's being asked.'

3) When things seem to be going wrong you can say:
   a) 'I knew it wouldn't be easy but I'll keep at it.'
   b) 'Don't give up, I'll try this other tack.'
   c) 'Keep calm, relax, breathe evenly.'
   d) 'OK, if I don't get promoted this time, I'll get promoted next time.'

4) What you can tell yourself when it is all over:

If it was successful:

   a) 'That was really good, I managed it.'
   b) 'Well done, you showed them what you were made of.'

If you were unsuccessful:

   a) 'Well I did my best, I need a bit more experience, maybe I'm not ready for governor yet.'
   b) 'You can't win them all.'
   c) 'If I work out what I did wrong I might be able to do better next time.'
   d) 'That's their loss, they didn't promote me.'

These are just examples of self-talk sentences – each person has to work out their own. It is important that you work out positive self-talk sentences and do not let negative self-talk dominate your thinking. When you see these tactics written down they may seem artificial but our thoughts and sensations affect both our physical and mental well-being. It is not what happens to us, but the way we think and interpret it, that makes us feel sad and uptight and which can have physical consequences; thus it is important that you get control of the 'negative noise' which is going on in your head.

Summary

Stress is part and parcel of many occupations. Some occupations are more stressful than others and indeed it would appear that being a prison officer is one of the more stressful. The level and nature of stress varies from institution to institution. The nature of stress experienced by any individual is determined partly by the nature of the work but also by the position in the organisation. The stresses experienced by a governor are different from those experienced by basic grade officers. The effects of stress can be wide-ranging. It may affect physical health and psychological health. In addition, it may lead to friction at work and trouble at home. The effects of stress are pervasive and it is important to learn how to prevent it happening and how to manage stress when it does happen. The skills of stress management are effective but they require practice. It is no use waiting until the stressful experience occurs and then trying out the techniques. It is important to become skilful before you find yourself under stress.

Chapter thirteen

Giving evidence in court

Dealing with criminals on a day-to-day basis, it is not surprising that prison staff sometimes have to give evidence in court. Prison staff may witness all sorts of criminal activities during their working lives from drug abuse and assaults through homosexual rape, fire-raising, malicious damage and hostage-taking.

There can be many difficulties in giving evidence properly. The court case may be held a long time after the event when memories have faded. The experience of going into a court can produce anxiety which can in turn lead to confusion; cross-examination can be intimidating. Many officers find the experience of going to court daunting. Not only that, if a conviction does not follow the court appearance, the morale of the officer and his or her colleagues can drop. There are ways in which the experience can be made less unnerving and there are ways in which evidence can be presented with greater skill.

In this chapter, we describe the court process and what is expected of a witness. We look at some of the ways in which you can reduce the worry about going to court and examine some of the methods which lawyers use in cross-examination to make you feel unsettled.

To learn how to cope with a court appearance, it is important to understand the function of a court. You may feel that this is obvious: it is to find out what happened, but the reality is less simple than that. In the United Kingdom and the United States, courts operate on the 'adversarial system', that is, a court case is a contest between two sides in which one side is trying to show that their evidence is much stronger than that of the other side. Did prisoner X set fire to his cell? Was prisoner Y selling drugs to other inmates? Did prisoner Z assault you? It is not the truth of these propositions that matters. What is important is the quality of the evidence put forward by the competing sides to support their own case.

Despite the fact that British witnesses swear to tell the truth, the whole truth and nothing but the truth, discovering the truth is not the primary function of the courts. To most people this may appear to be a peculiar notion. Nonetheless, various legal authorities support it. Sir David Napley – a noted Queen's Councel – stated: 'The criminal trial is not the pursuit of the whole truth, whether it be scientific or factual truth.' He is not alone in this view. In his autobiography, John Mortimer, barrister and creator of Rumpole of the Bailey, argued: 'A British criminal trial is not primarily an investigation to discover the truth, although truth may sometimes be disinterred by chance. A criminal trial is a test of the prosecution evidence, a procedure to discover if the case against the accused person can be proved beyond all reasonable doubt.'

How does this come about? How is the search for truth frustrated? Two aspects of court proceedings seem to be important: first, the rules of evidence that apply in court; and second, the stereotypes that apply to accused people.

Rules of evidence are designed to exclude evidence that might be unfair or unsafe. Evidence may be excluded – evidence which would lead straight to the truth – because it is thought to be unfair to the defendant. Two simple examples are the rules which apply to 'hearsay evidence' and the rules which apply to confessions. Hearsay evidence, that is, evidence which has not been directly observed by a witness, e.g. 'She told me she'd seen him with a knife', is not accepted. This is because the person who observed the evidence cannot be cross-examined. Their evidence cannot be tested. Thus, evidence that may be totally accurate, detailed and truthful, is excluded because it is unsafe.

Equally, with evidence obtained by confession, the presiding judge can exclude the evidence if he considers that the confession was obtained by threats or inducement. It is vital that these safeguards exist, but it is clear that they may affect the evaluation of the truth.

The search for truth may be affected in other ways, through the operation of subtle and less obvious processes in the court system. Courts are designed to process guilty people and most people who appear in court are found guilty. In the English magistrates' court system, for example, over 90 per cent of cases are resolved with either a plea of guilt or a verdict of guilty. The innocent are rare in the court system. Thus stereotypes develop: 'There's no smoke without fire', 'If he didn't commit this offence he's probably done some other'. While the stated assumption is that all defendants are innocent until proved guilty, in a system designed to process the guilty, the opposite may apply: you are guilty unless you can prove otherwise.

Thus, if you go to court to give evidence you should realise that the court is not fundamentally concerned about truth, guilt or innocence. The court is concerned with the quality of the evidence. It is important to realise that in the combative atmosphere of our court system you may be asked about your evidence – not to find out the truth – but perhaps to obscure and confuse the truth. If you are to provide useful and accurate evidence then you must develop the skills of presenting evidence in a clear fashion. You must learn to deal with tactics of lawyers who may wish to frustrate this goal.

Going to court

Courtrooms are formal settings with their own strict rules. To be an effective witness, it is important to be aware of and to become familiar with these rules. The best way of getting to grips with them, and over-coming any anxiety about a court appearance, is to observe a court case. As a witness to the facts – a witness who talks about what they saw and what they heard – you are not allowed to watch the trial until after you have given your evidence. But you can go into the public gallery during another trial. If you go to see a trial you will get used to the unfamiliar courtroom environment. It is an environment which is the day-to-day work-place of the major participants in the proceedings: the judge, the lawyers, the courtroom officials and perhaps even the defendant himself. They will all feel at home there. It is often only the poor witness who feels unfamiliar.

When you go to give evidence you must do your best to fit in with the conventions of the court. One important convention is the way in which you dress. Wigs, dark suits and dark gowns are standard dress for the legal participants in the court room drama. Research on witnesses shows that those who dress in dark, conservative clothes are considered to be serious and knowledgeable. Their evidence is given more authority and is taken more seriously. If you wear items such as flashy jewellery, a Mickey Mouse watch or a political badge, there is a risk that you will offend or distract someone of a conservative disposition. If this happens, your evidence may not be given the importance it deserves.

Giving evidence

When you enter the witness box you will be asked to take the oath or to affirm. This is when you will find out how your voice sounds in the courtroom. Courtrooms can be noisy places so it is important that you speak out so that the jury can hear what you have to say. But most important, if you speak in a firm and assured manner, your evidence may be taken more seriously.

When giving evidence, there is one particular courtroom convention that often confuses people. In court it is normal for a witness to speak directly to the judge even though the question has been asked by one of the other lawyers. You have to overcome the lifelong habit of replying to the person who asked you the question. The normal rules of conversation do not apply. The questioner may be looking away from you, be reading their notes on the other side of the courtroom, or watching the response of the jury. How can you deal with this without getting confused or anxious? The best procedure is to stand in the witness box so that you face the judge. You will then have to turn at the waist to receive the questions and then turn back to give your reply to the judge. This approach has two advantages: first, you are sticking to the convention of replying to the judge; and second, it allows you to control the length of your replies.

Controlling your reply is important. Advocates are trained to keep control of the witnesses' answers. They do this by using body language; for example, by using silence and lack of eye contact to make you say more, particularly when you are contradicting yourself or giving unclear evidence. On the other hand, they may try to keep your answers short by coming close to you, demanding your attention and interrupting your statements. The technique of turning from counsel to judge and back again allows you to maintain control over the rhythm of questions. It gives you time to think, and it gives you the chance to present your evidence in a more expert fashion.

Types of evidence-giving

Not all evidence-giving is the same. Evidence is presented in three distinct phases: examination-in-chief, cross-examination and re-examination. In examination-in-chief you will be examined by the advocate who called you to give evidence. He would not have called you if your evidence was not useful to his side of the argument, so examination-in-chief is usually straightforward. The advocate will take you through all the information which supports his case in as clear, concise and convincing a manner as possible.

Examination-in-chief is made easier by good preparation. Immediately after the offence, if at all possible, you should write down what you saw or heard. We know from research that the memories of witnesses can play tricks on them. It is not simply that witnesses forget things; they often reconstruct what happened in a distorted way. These distortions can be dramatic. After a few months you may begin to remember that the prisoner dropped the knife immediately after he had stabbed your colleague whereas, in reality, he was found to still have it in his possession when he was caught. If your evidence becomes distorted in this way, then a good counsel will pick up the differences between your evidence and the evidence of other witnesses. By finding the differences they can discredit all of your evidence. If you write things down immediately after the offence, then these distortions are less likely to occur. If the police take a statement, try to get a copy of it. If you are a particularly important witness – say you were taken hostage and you are giving evidence at the trial of the perpetrators – then counsel who is calling you should talk to you about your evidence. He should tell you what questions he intends to ask and you should tell him about the parts of your evidence which you are clear about and the parts which are unclear.

Cross-examination follows immediately after examination-in-chief and is conducted by the opposing counsel. Cross-examination is designed to evaluate the quality of your evidence. It is designed to reveal inconsistencies in your statements, distortions in your memory and misinterpretations of what you witnessed. Cross-examination may also be aimed at reducing your credibility as a witness, and thereby, the credibility of your evidence. How can this be achieved?

Dangers in cross-examination

Lawyers have many different tricks which they can use to trap the unwary during cross-examination. We will look at four common ploys.

Jumping

If you are looking settled in the witness-box and giving your evidence in a clear and competent manner, the counsel may try to unsettle you using the technique of 'jumping'. Counsels can ask for evidence in any order which they choose. They may start by asking you what you were doing before you were taken hostage. They may then ask about what happened on the fifth day of your captivity, then ask about your experience in the prison service. After that they could go back to ask you about what happened on the third day of your captivity. 'Jumping' is designed to confuse you. If counsel succeeds in confusing you, he can discredit your evidence so that it will be taken less seriously by the jury. How can you combat this tactic? There are two ways. First, be prepared. Rehearse your evidence in advance. Work out where you might be tripped up. Work out how you will answer the tricky questions. Second, take time to think before answering your questions. Do not be bullied into replying before you have time to think about your answer.

Interrupting

Counsels are taught that they must keep control of witnesses' answers. One technique which they use to keep control is interruption. They interrupt you before you have time to explain what you have said. This can change the whole meaning of your evidence. There are two ways in which you can deal with this. The first tactic is to explain your answer before you give it, for instance:

Counsel: 'Is it possible that you made a mistake when you said that my client was the hooded man with the knife in his hand?'

Witness: 'I have known him for five years and therefore it is very unlikely that I'm mistaken, but it is possible.'

Witness: 'It is possible, but I have known him for five years and it is very unlikely that I'm mistaken.'

In the first example, it is difficult to cut you off before you have explained your answer fully. In the second case, if you had been cut off after 'It is possible' then the sense of your evidence becomes quite different.

The second technique is to use the trick of saying you have a number of points to describe:

Witness: 'There are three things that I noticed, one . . ., two . . ., three . . .'. If you cannot be sure in advance how many points you want to make, just guess and if you are wrong, finish by saying: 'My third point is covered by the other two'.

In desperation, if you feel that you are being interrupted to an intolerable extent, you can quickly turn to the judge and say, 'I think the shortness of my answers may mislead the court. Can I reply in more detail?' Witnesses have rights too.

The 'prefactory remark'

Another device which can be used during cross-examination is the 'prefactory remark'. This is when counsel makes a statement before asking you a question. If you fail to comment on the statement and merely reply to the question, it may appear that you agree with the statement. This statement may be used during the summing up of the case. An example of this tactic might be where counsel defending a client appears to be asking you about your experience, but begins:

> Counsel: 'I am sure we all agree that my client did very little serious damage. Tell me, have you seen this sort of incident before during your service?'

The counsel's first statement has got nothing to do with the question. If you merely reply to the question you may appear to agree that his 'client did very little serious damage'. Where this tactic is employed, begin by disagreeing with the statement then answer the question. If you do not disagree, it may appear that you actually agree with the statement

The 'slippery slope'

The final technique we want to look at is called the 'slippery slope'. In essence, the lawyer tries to get you to change your evidence by getting you to agree to gradual changes in the meaning of your statement. This is a subtle approach. The lawyer uses stealth in order to trap you into changes. Here is an example.

The lawyer might start off by flattering you to make you relax. Then he gets you to answer lots of short questions so you get into the habit of responding quickly without thinking. Finally, he gets you to change your evidence.

> Counsel: 'Senior Officer Brown, would you like to tell the Court how many years you have worked in the prison service?'
>
> Witness: 'I have fifteen years' service'
>
> Counsel: 'Could you tell the Court what profession you pursued before you joined the prison service?'
>
> Witness: 'I was a sergeant in the military police.'

Counsel: 'You must know a lot about crime and criminals?'
Witness: 'I hope that I do.'
Counsel: 'It is my belief that the Court is privileged to have someone who has given so much service to his country here to give evidence today. I am sure we will value your evidence with the merit that it obviously deserves.'
Witness: 'Thank you.'
Counsel: 'You have fifteen years' service?'
Witness: 'Yes.'
Counsel: 'On the day of the incident you started your shift at one o'clock?'
Witness: 'Yes.'
Counsel: 'You had a meal break at five o'clock?'
Witness: 'Yes.'
Counsel: 'You saw my client come downstairs with a knife in his hand and a hood over his head?'
Witness: 'Yes.'
Counsel: 'There were 150 prisoners in the hall at the time. You would agree that there is always a remote possibility that it wasn't my client but someone else who had the hood over his head?'
Witness: 'Yes, I suppose there is a remote possibility.'
Counsel: 'There was a lot happening that night. There was noise, smoke and fire. So there is a chance that the person you saw with the hood was someone who looked like my client?'
Witness: 'Yes, there is a chance.'
Counsel: 'I understand you were injured that night – you are fully recovered now I trust. You were injured and a lot was happening around you. So with all that to contend with there must have been a reasonable chance that someone of the same build as my client, someone wearing the same prison clothes, could be mistaken for my client? I'm not saying you were mistaken, but that there is a reasonable chance.'
Witness: 'Yes, you may be correct.'
Counsel: 'So we are agreed, Senior Officer Brown, that there is a reasonable chance that it was someone else of the same build who was wearing the hood.'

So the officer has moved down the slippery slope. He started by agreeing that there was a remote possibility that he had mistakenly identified the accused. In the end he agreed that there was a reasonable chance that someone else was wearing the hood. You may believe that you would not succumb to such a tactic, but if you are in the strange atmosphere of the court, if you are softened up by the flattery of the counsel, if you are lured into responding with short quick responses, you too could succumb.

The cross-examination is over but you cannot relax. There is one more stage. The final part of the evidential process is re-examination. Re-examination is carried out by the counsel who called the witness. His goal is to correct any misperceptions which emerged during cross-examination. During re-examination the counsel will ask questions to emphasise the central features of your evidence, the features which he wishes the jury to remember.

Summary

Many prison officers can go through their careers without having to appear in court, others will appear regularly during their careers. Whether you appear once or several times, it is important, for yourself and the prison service, that you present your evidence in a clear and professional manner.

Index

aggression: causes 45–53, 104; gains from aggression 45; influence of feelings and thoughts 46–8, 51–3, 104; influence of others behaviour 49–51; influence of surroundings 48–9; learning to use aggression 43–5; types of aggression 42–3

AIDS: and prostitution 26; controlling AIDS 75–6; definition 68; detecting AIDS 71, 73; getting AIDS 68–9; HIV positive 68–9, 72–3; in prison 76–7; protection against AIDS 73–4, 74–5; risky behaviour 69–71

alcohol: and criminal behaviour 27–41; nature and effects 29–30; use by prison staff 40

anxiety 60–1, 93–4; see also psychological disturbance

assertion 86–8

body language: and assertion 87; and listening 82–3; see also communication skills

communication skills: acceptance 85–6; assertion 86–8; coping with face-to-face violence 106; giving orders 88–9; handling requests 89; importance in prison 79, 80; in violent situations 108–10; listening skills 82–6; observation skills 80–2, 103–4; reflection 84; report writing 89–90; self-disclosure 84–5

courts: dangers in cross-examination 141–5; giving evidence 140; mode of dress 139; truth and justice 138–9; types of evidence 140–1

criminal behaviour: costs and benefits 13–15; crises and negative life events 11–12; current living circumstances 11; different causes 8, 12–13; early environment 9–10; heredity 10; role of alcohol 35–6; role of drugs 27–41; situational factors 12; socio-economic status 10; sex offenders see offences

depression 61–2; see psychological disturbance

drugs: alcohol 29–30; amphetamine 32–3; barbiturates 33–4; benzodiazepines 33; cannabis 34–5; coming off drugs 36–8; drug use and AIDS 70; help for drug users 38–9; heroin 31–2; solvents 35; tobacco 30–1; types of drugs 28–35; withdrawal symptoms 37–8

giving evidence in courts 140–5
giving orders 88–9

handling requests 89
homosexuality 23–4; and AIDS 70
hostage-taking: coping with 117–20,
   120–1, 121–2; first on the scene
   116–17; history 112–13; methods
   of resolution 113–15;
   psychological effects of 120–2

observation skills 80–2, 103–4

psychological disturbance: anxiety
   60–1, 93–4; assisting prisoners
   with 94–5, 97, 98, 98–100; brain
   injury 100–1; depression 61–2,
   96–7; describing 92–3; effects of
   imprisonment 55–6; effects of
   lack of communication 64–6;
   effects of loss of control 55–6;
   effects of loss of family 56–8;
   effects of loss of models 60; lack
   of stimulation 58–9; learning
   difficulties 98–100; self-injury
   63–4, 97–8; suicide 62–3
psychology: or common sense 2;
   application in prison 2–5; what is
   it? 1–5

relaxation 94–5
report writing 89–90

self injury 63–4

sexual behaviour: development of
   sexual interests 16–18; differences
   in sexual attitudes 18–19;
   influence of early experience 17;
   influence of sexual fantasies 17;
   see also sexual offences
sex offences: causes 16–18;
   homosexuality 23–4; incest 22–3;
   indecent exposure 19–20; offences
   against children 21–2; prostitution
   24–5; sexual assault and rape 20–1
sexual offenders in prison 25–6
stress: and criminal behaviour
   11–12; coping with 128–36;
   effects of violence 110–11; effects
   on family 125; effects on work
   performance 126; following
   hostage-taking 120–2; managing
   131–5; physical effects 125;
   prevention 129–31; psychological
   effects 124–5; stress in prisons
   126–8
structure of book 5–7
suicide in prison 62–3

violence: avoiding 102–3; effects on
   staff 110–11; facing aggressive
   people 106; motives 104;
   precautions against 104–6;
   preventing escalation 106–8;
   see also aggression

Printed in the United States
67491LVS00002B/46